# WELL MADE

## WELL DONE

## DOUG BURRIER

WHEN IT'S TIME FOR SOMETHING NEW
DIFFERENT.LY
publishing

Published 2022 by Different.ly Publishing
PO Box 176
Cave Spring, Georgia 30124
www.different.ly

ISBN: 978-1-7334021-2-5
First Edition.
Printed in the United States of America

"Well done, my good and faithful servant. You have been faithful in handling this small amount, so now I will give you many more responsibilities. Let's celebrate together!

— Jesus

# CONTENTS

# INTRODUCTION

If we are making bicycles, we know what an operational bicycle looks like. It has wheels, brakes, drive and steering systems, and, most importantly, a comfortable seat. Before we ship it out, we can test it to make sure it is operational. How do you do that with disciples?

One of the most common disciple-making questions is, "What does a disciple look like?" I hear it at every conference and seminar, and in almost every private workshop. It makes sense. We want to make disciples, but how do we measure success? When are they done? When do we move them on?

The problem is that God's Word does not give us a checklist. We know that disciples should follow God. We know they should be sold out. And over time, we have come up with some Christian phrases to help define our goal. Do any of these sound familiar?

- *True disciples are fully devoted followers of Christ.*
- *True disciples exhibit the character of Christ.*

- *True disciples multiply, making disciples themselves.*
- *True disciples are servants of God, the church, and the world.*

Each catchphrase attempts to answer the question "What does a finished disciple look like?" And though each captures some truth about a well-made disciple, none can stand on its own as a measure of success. In fact, some of them cannot be measured at all.

For example, how do we know when a disciple is a fully devoted follower? What does "fully devoted" mean? The words "disciple" and "follower" have the same meaning. Why are we adding the phrase "fully devoted"? Are there degrees of following? If so, how do we know when someone reaches the goal of being fully devoted?

If we say that a true disciple exhibits the character of Christ, we are left to ask, "What is the character of Christ?" Did Jesus's disciples reflect His character? Did Jesus succeed in His disciple making as Peter denied Him? How much time do you have to spend with a person to truly know their character? Evaluating the character of a disciple is too subjective and complex to be a useful measure of success in disciple making.

We can measure how many disciples a disciple makes. But measuring success by multiplication alone fails if we only focus on quantity without considering quality. It is true, well-made disciples will most likely make well-made disciples. But poorly made disciples always make poorly made disciples. Measuring multiplication is simply not enough. We must ask, "Are the many who are being made being well made?"

We can measure if a disciple serves. But using service as a measure of success fails because people can serve for the wrong reasons. Measuring service can quickly lead to performance-based discipleship. And measuring service does not take into account spiritual maturity.

So how can you measure your success in making disciples?

> *Your success in disciple making can be measured by how many disciples continue to follow God for the right reasons and navigate the unknowns long after your influence fades.*

This description of success recognizes the truth that well-made disciples will multiply. It establishes a goal. We should be making disciples, lots of them. But it also ties our success to the quality of each disciple we make by establishing three more goals:

- *Each disciple should know what to do and why to do it.*
- *Each disciple should be able to stand on their own two feet.*
- *Each disciple should be able to face the unknowns of life with confidence.*

A well-made disciple knows what to do and why to do it. He is prepared. He has consumed God's Word. A well-made disciple knows the promises, rewards, and blessings associated with following God's design. He has seen the warnings, downfalls, and dangers of not following God. He understands how and why to apply each truth to his decisions. He understands the right reason to do the right thing. A well-made disciple understands the why.

A well-made disciple applies God's truths on her own. She is a self-sustaining, sold-out follower of God. She is a confident self-starter. She has experienced the value of applying God's truths to her circumstances and decisions. A well-made disciple succeeds, with each success fueling the desire for continued success.

And a well-made disciple faces new challenges and situations with confidence. He is skilled at connecting God's truths to see the bigger picture. He extends discreet truths to new situations. When a well-made disciple faces the unknown, he knows that nothing is unknown to God. He understands the big picture of God's desires, character, and values. A well-made disciple applies his understanding when he cannot find a direct answer to a decision he faces.

These three goals of success in disciple making are not arbitrary. You can find them cover to cover in the Bible, again and again, as God makes disciples. Paul, one of the most prolific writers on the Christian life, said it this way.

*All Scripture is inspired by God and is useful to teach us what is true and to make us realize what is wrong in our lives. It corrects us when we are wrong and teaches us to do what is right. [17]God uses it to prepare and equip his people to do every good work.*
—2 Timothy 3:16–17

*Finally, dear brothers and sisters, we urge you in the name of the Lord Jesus to live in a way that pleases God, as we have taught you. You live this way already, and we encourage you to do so even more.*
    —1 Thessalonians 4:1

*But if you have doubts about whether or not you should eat something, you are sinning if you go ahead and do it. For you are not following your convictions. If you do anything you believe is not right, you are sinning.*
    —Romans 14:23

Do you see it? Paul tells us to know and understand, do it independently, and face the unknown with confidence, acting on faith. Jesus said it this way.

*"You are truly my disciples if you remain faithful to my teachings. 32And you will know the truth, and the truth will set you free."*
    —John 8:31–32

*"All who love me will do what I say. My Father will love them, and we will come and make our home with each of them. 24Anyone who doesn't love me will not obey me. And remember, my words are not my own. What I am telling you is from the Father who sent me. 25I am telling you these things now while I am still with you. 26But when the Father sends the Advocate as my representative—that is, the Holy Spirit—he will teach you everything and will remind you of everything I have told you.*

*27"I am leaving you with a gift—peace of mind and heart. And the peace I give is a gift the world cannot give. So don't be troubled or afraid. Remember what I told you: I am going away, but I will come back to you again."*
—John 14:23–28

Jesus taught his disciples to know the truth and showed them the value of those truths: freedom. He pushed them to do it on their own. And Jesus told them to face the unknown with confidence and faith in the Holy Spirit.

Again and again, God's Word reveals the three measures of success. His faithful followers in the Old and New Testaments were self-sustaining, sold-out followers. They knew what to do and why to do it. They knew the promises, rewards, and blessings for doing things God's way. And His faithful followers were able to connect God's words to see the big picture. They faced and navigated new challenges and situations with faith and confidence.

Well-made followers understand the why, do it on their own, and navigate the unknown with confidence. One measure of success is not enough. Disciples need to succeed in all three areas to find lasting success. If we put it in a Venn diagram, it would look this way.

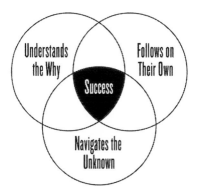

Your lasting, successful investment is found at the intersection of all three measures. Anything outside the intersection is not a complete success. If any leg of this three-legged stool is short, the disciple's life will be lopsided and, often, tipped toward failure.

So we have a driving statement of success:

*Your success in disciple making can be measured by how many disciples continue to follow God for the right reasons and navigate the unknowns long after your influence fades.*

And we have three goals for each disciple we make:

- *He understands the "why";*
- *He does it on his own; and*
- *He faces and navigates the unknown with confidence.*

Now we can begin measuring our success in each goal. And that is important because our success in disciple making is essential to the disciples' success. Our success in making leads to their success. And their success is our success.

So how do we know if we are succeeding? We walk with them, listen to them, and watch what they do. It makes sense. After all, disciples do specific, measurable things and exhibit specific, quantifiable qualities. Even Jesus and Paul stressed doing. There is no doubt, healthy followers do healthy things. But measuring success by "dos" gets messy because people who are not fully devoted followers do these same things. Lost people can be loving, charitable, and peaceful. Dead Christians can attend, tithe, and serve. We see it every day in ministry and life.

This is why we add qualifiers like "fully devoted" and "true disciple" to our definitions of success. We know there is a difference between the doing of a true disciple and the doing of most Christians. But we also know that disciples "doing" is a measure of success. The key to measuring a disciple's success in doing is to ask, "Why are they doing what they are doing?"

For example, if a person does something because God convicts him that it is good, he follows God. If he does not do something because of God, he follows God. But when people do things because of social pressure, pastor pressure, or legalism, they are not following God. A well-made disciple is motivated by the value of following and applying God's truths. He is inspired by God's design, and he is following God's plan.

Asking, "Why do they do these things?" allows us to measure whether we have made disciples or robots. A well-made disciple understands the "why." That is our first measure of success in disciple making. The second measure is "Will they do it on their own?"

Walking beside a disciple is the only way to help him discover the "why" to do things. Walking behind him is the only way to know if he will do it on his own. Jesus did this with his disciples as he observed them processing and applying God's truths. He did this when he put them in challenging situations. He did this when he sent them out on their own.

One of the most common definitions of integrity is doing the right thing when no one is watching. In the same way, you have succeeded in making a disciple when they follow on their own when they are solely accountable to God. A well-made disciple does it on their own when no one is around. That is our second measure of success in disciple making. The third measure is "How do they navigate the unknown?"

Conceptually, the Bible is complete. But practically, the Bible is far from complete. Each generation, every era, faces new challenges and opportunities. A New Testament believer never had to ask, "What college should I attend?" because there were no colleges. Before there were automobiles, no one asked, "Economy or sporty? Which is the wise buy?" Disciples face all kinds of questions that are not answered in the Bible, from "Who should I vote for?" to "Who should I marry?" These questions are the great unknowns. These questions can only be answered by tying God's conceptual truths together and connecting the dots of His words. Asking, "Have they learned to learn?" is another way of phrasing our third measure.

Walking along the way lets you know if they get the

"why." Walking behind them lets you know if they will do it on their own. Watching them navigate the unknowns lets you know they have learned to learn. When these three things come together, you have successfully made a disciple.

The tests of our success in this book are by no means exhaustive, but each illustrates these three measures. Hopefully, each example will provide a context for you to answer, "What does a disciple look like?" and, "Did I really make a disciple?"

In the final chapters, we will look at some practical ways to help them get the why, do it on their own, and navigate the unknowns of life. For now, let's go drop a disciple on a deserted island.

# CHAPTER 1
# COCONUTS

Wilson woke up feeling the warm sun on his back and the grit of sand in his mouth. It did not take long for him to realize he was stranded, alone on a deserted island. Wilson did what anyone would do. Within seconds, he was praying for help. Within hours, Wilson was working on a signal fire. Within days, he had gathered large stones and spelled out "help" on the beach. But help did not come.

So Wilson did what anyone would do next: he searched for food. He was so happy when he found coconuts! He gathered up ten and headed back to camp. But then Wilson did something that most people would not do. Wilson picked up a coconut, walked toward the shore, set the coconut on a rock, looked to the sky, and said, "Thank you, God, for providing for me. This coconut is yours. I love you."

As the days passed, Wilson continued to give God coconut offerings. No one was watching. No one was passing the coconut plate. No one was trying to fund a new parking lot with coconuts. It was just Wilson and God. When the pile grew large, he never thought, "This is stupid. This is wasteful. God does not need any more of my coconuts. Clearly, he has enough." He just kept giving coconuts. One coconut and one thankful prayer for every ten.

One day, while sipping on a coconut, Wilson looked toward the shore and saw God's pile of coconuts. Without thinking, he said, "God, it would be so cool if you would drop fire from heaven like you did with Gideon and consume my offering. The angel didn't need the meal that Gideon prepared, and you don't need this big pile of coconuts. But they are yours. That would be so cool!" As he finished, poof! Fire flashed down from heaven and consumed the pile. Wilson went nuts. He was still dancing, singing, and running around, whooping praises to God as the sun set on the horizon.

Sunrise and a cool breeze woke Wilson the next day. His smile broadened as the scent of his burnt offering wafted through the camp. And, of course, Wilson went out to collect his daily coconuts. He gathered ten, kept nine, and set one down on the charred rock among the ashes. Then he sat down and waited. No fire. Thirty days later, with the offering pile big again, Wilson wondered, "Why? Why no fire?" but he never questioned God's love for him. He did not wonder if he had done something to offend God. His faith in God, his adoration of God, did not change. Instead, Wilson remembered the Old and New Testament followers' failures when they worshiped the provision instead of the provider. He remembered that God is the God who gives and takes fire. Fire or no fire, Wilson was going to remain thankful and tithe.

A few days later, he noticed something green among the ashes. A coconut, half-buried, had something green on it. Then Wilson saw another coconut with green. The coconuts were spouting among the ashes! He remembered God's truth that God will multiply our offerings. He remembered God's words in Malachi saying that God poured out blessings on those who tithe. Wilson stood up and prayed, "Thank you for not burning this pile. Thank you for multiplying it." He was overcome with wonder at God's promises and God's practical design of this planet. He recognized the God who brings sprouts from ashes. He worshipped the God who multiplies physical offerings and spiritual offerings. That moment was as powerful for Wilson as the fire from heaven.

Days later, God spoke quietly in Wilson's heart: "Don't collect coconuts for ten days. Instead, eat the coconuts from the top of the pile. Nine each day for ten days. And do not tithe." Wilson obeyed. He was not worried about God telling him to do something that was against God's law. Instead, Wilson remembered God telling Hosea to marry a prostitute.[1] He remembered David eating the bread of the altar.[2] He knew that God's laws are made for man, not for God. So Wilson trusted what he heard and ate from the pile.

When a storm ravaged the island, taking all but seven coconuts out to sea, Wilson still gave a tenth. He needed nine to stay full, but he knew that his needs did not over-rule the truths of the tithe. God gets the first, and God will supply the rest. Wilson's stomach was growling as he gave his last coconut offering, but he did not complain. Instead, Wilson remembered the widow giving her last coin.[3] In the morning, he noticed new coconuts on the tree and remembered Jesus multiplying the fish and the bread. What a journey he was having!

Wilson's days went on filled with far more than collecting and tithing coconuts. Through it all, Wilson applied the truth that God was the provider. When he needed shelter, Wilson talked with God about building a shelter because he remembered God giving Solomon wisdom in all things. When his hut fell down, Wilson rested in the truth that God is not only the provider of coconuts but also encouragement and learning. He knew he had a God-given ability to learn from his mistakes. He remembered that God could use all of his failures and successes to His glory. And on that day, Wilson remembered Paul's words about being a living sacrifice, an offering holy and acceptable to God.[4] He was reminded that if he offered himself to God, God would take care of him. He was reminded of Jesus's words telling him not to worry about material things. He remembered Jesus's promise that His Father would provide.[5] And God was providing for him. Wilson did not need to be rescued. He was thriving with God.

Wilson was a well-made disciple. He was doing the right things for the right reasons on his own and facing the unknowns of his experience with confidence.

We see it in his story. Wilson understood the "why" behind giving. At some point, he learned the simple truth that we should give one-tenth of our increase. Wilson also knew enough about God to know that God does not need his coconut. Wilson understood that the tithe is more about him than it is about God. He knew tithing was about being thankful. It is about gratitude. It is about trusting God for the next coconut. So Wilson gave God a coconut.

Wilson did it on his own when there was no one to please, no one to impress, no needs to support, and no plate in which to place his coconut. No one was there. No one was aware. But Wilson got it! Tithing is worship at a profoundly personal level. He understood the immediate value of gratitude and the long-term value of fighting materialism. God's values behind tithing became Wilson's. And giving coconuts became Wilson's own unstoppable practice.

Wilson connected a variety of God's truths to face the unknown with confidence. He saw the bigger picture. Discipleship had never taught him to build a hut, but Wilson knew that God could provide ideas and inspiration if he would offer God his mind. Never before had Wilson run out of coconuts. But when he did, he could trust God because he had already experienced God's promise of provision. The many truths of God's provision fueled God's simple command to give a tenth. Wilson understood God's physical and spiritual economics. He had connected the dots between the thankful tithe and God as a provider in all things. He knew he could not out-give God, and Wilson knew his greatest gift was to give himself to God. Wilson had extended God's truths about tithing into other areas of his life!

Of course, Wilson is fictional. He is only a placeholder for that disciple you are making. But can you imagine a church full of Wilsons? Can you imagine no money problems? Can you imagine wise, patient, grateful givers who are looking for the fire and the sprouts?

If you want a church full of coconut givers, remember that Wilson's success did not just happen. It was a journey of learning and applying truth. It was a journey to discover the value of tithing. And it was a journey of trust and confidence built upon many different truths about God's provision and materialism.

Wilson did not magically become a coconut giver. Wilson was well made. Someone sacrificed and invested in Wilson. Someone wanted Wilson to thrive and enjoy the abundant life God promised. Someone exposed him to the truths about tithing. Someone helped him discover the values, the why, behind tithing and giving. Someone pushed Wilson to apply what he learned. Wilson became a coconut giver as he experienced God's increasing blessings.

*Wilson was ready to do it on his own for the right reasons because someone had succeeded in making him a disciple of God.*

Is your church full of coconut givers? You may already know the answer, but if not, take this test: stop passing the plate. Do not explain it. Just stop passing the plate. Stop the reminders. Stop the public display and all the verbal stretching that goes along with making it part of your worship service. Stop the fundraising and watch what happens. It sounds bold, but it will give you a quick measure of your success.

Our church did this exact thing about fifteen years ago. Like everyone else, the offering was a standard part of our worship. But no one was worshipping as the plates passed by. Our leadership team had this aha moment when we realized passing the plates was a lot like marketing. It was a constant reminder for people to give. And to be honest, we needed the money. You get it. We had built a machine that needed to be fed, and the people's wallets were the feeding troughs. But suddenly, it felt cheap. None of us got into ministry to become fundraisers. None of us wanted to look at people as dollars. Sure, we knew it was healthy for them to give, but ultimately, we needed their money. Getting them to tithe had become more about us and less about their lives. What had we become?

So we stopped passing the plates. The results were both expected and surprising. As you would expect, we immediately had a new budget—a lower budget. Those who only gave when they were reminded, prodded, or pushed stopped giving. What we did not expect was that sixty percent of our families figured it out and kept giving. We were encouraged until we talked to them. Most of the sixty percent were giving out of obligation. Either they were raised in church and knew it was the "right thing to do" or they were afraid of what might happen to them if they did not give. The sixty percent were not giving for the right reasons. Worse, very few families who gave were tithing. They were only giving what they could afford, dropping God trinkets along the way.

It was heartbreaking. Our leaders were giving because of the value we had seen in God's truths. We were living proof that ninety percent was more than enough. We were experiencing the blessings, freedom, and miracles that tithers always experience. We gave when it hurt. We gave out of a full heart. We trusted God to provide. It was fun to give. It was exciting to trust God and see him provide. We were coconut givers, but clearly we had not made coconut givers. So we started the long trek to making disciples. We stopped ministries, cut our salaries, and learned to live on what God provided. We never passed the plate again and taught the real reasons for the tithe. We exposed them to God's instructions on tithing. We focused on the values of tithing: gratitude, anti-materialism, trust, and self-sacrifice. All in all, it took a couple of years to "remake" ourselves as coconut givers.

We also began strategically helping people to become coconut followers in all areas of their lives. We began to measure our success in disciple making across the board. And it worked. Fifteen years later, we rarely talk or teach about tithing. Most of our people have spent time becoming prepared, confident, and skilled followers of God. Along the way, they have seen his tithing truths, apply them, and follow him. Today, ninety percent of our people tithe (not just give), and they are better for it.

It is important to note here that coconut givers are not the target. The target is coconut followers. The important thing is that they are followers, not that they are doing what a follower would do. A well-made disciple has been transformed by the renewing of his mind. He knows the truth, understands the whys, applies the truth, and extends the truth to other aspects of living. And he has a relationship with God, a relationship that thrives without you or me.

Measuring success in disciple making can seem complicated. You can't just drop your church members or disciples off on deserted islands. (There is a lawsuit in that!) We will talk more about how you can get them there and measure their success in the final chapters of this book. For now, let us know that a disciple who tithes a coconut on a deserted island was successfully made. And let us head off to another example of well-made disciples.

# CHAPTER 2
# UNEMPLOYMENT

I was driving home from a discipleship group when all of a sudden, KAPOW! A car slammed into me. In the blink of an eye, I was careening down a twenty-foot embankment toward a grove of trees and five months off work.

I love our church. I teach there. I lead there. But in those months, I could do none of that. I was gone, which worries every pastor I know. Will the church still be there when I get back? Will attendance have dropped? You know this feeling when you worry about what would happen if you had to be away from your job. But do you know what happened while I was gone? Nothing. There were no coups, no divisions, no problems—life went on, no one missed a beat. Nathanael and Seth, two emerging leaders, took over Sunday teaching. Tim, a great right-hand man, rose to the challenge of keeping the staff together. Greg, one of my best friends and one of my first successes in making a disciple, took over my discipleship groups.

Events went on. Missions got done. And the more I healed, the more I missed it all.

Nathanael and Seth would visit and tell me all the cool stuff that was happening. When I asked, "Is there anything you need help with?" they would reply, "Nope. You get well. Everyone is getting it done." Tim would check in on me, but his answer was the same: "Everything is good. Do your therapy. Get well." Greg excelled with my discipleship groups—they loved him and his different perspective. Discipleship leaders worked to challenge and help each other. The church grew. The bills got paid. Decisions got made. Problems got solved. Heck, they even refinanced the place while I was gone.

And an odd thing happened inside me: I started questioning whether I was needed. I wondered if I would have a job when this was over. My wife, Amber, spoke truth into my despair: "Doug, don't you realize that this is your legacy? Everything that you have ever dreamed of is coming true. These people don't need you. Discipleship has worked. This isn't your downfall. This is your success." Hard words to hear, but even in those words echoed the success of discipleship. My wife was practicing discipleship with me!

The truth was (and still is) that I was not needed for the work of Three Taverns to continue. These people not only maintained the status quo but also moved forward. They made new disciples and raised up new teachers. They expanded their leadership into new areas. And they did it without a hitch. The coolest part was that these folks were regular people. You expect a well-trained staff to pick up the slack and get through, but these people were ordinary people. Not one of them was a professional minister. Not one of them had been to seminary or leadership school. Their only qualification was being well-made disciples.

Unlike the coconut story, this story is not hypothetical. These disciples faced real challenges, real problems, and real questions with confidence and skill. Looking back, it is easy to see the third measure of success. They navigated the unknown by synthesizing many simple truths to make complex decisions. They walked independently and successfully. There was never a doubt in their minds that they would succeed in doing God's work. They had learned to learn. But what about the other two success factors?

Most often, if you see the third measure of success, the other two are already present. That was true with these disciples. They had been doing it and kept doing it on their own (success factor number two). They did not need to be pushed. They just picked up the ball and ran. They pursued the work of God in the church because they pursued the work of God in their own lives. They had already been given challenges. Like residents in a hospital, they had experienced success and failure along the way with those who made them disciples. They were more than ready to do it on their own.

With no direction, they banded together as a team of equals operating like the well-oiled body of Christ. They recognized the ones God had gifted to lead and followed them into the unknown. Everyone was humble. There were no power struggles. These disciples operated with unity and unanimity in every decision.

They did not vote or play politics as they talked, planned, and worked together. They were not seeking consensus like semi-confident people seek affirmation. They were not trying to get "buy-in." And they were not doing committees. What they were doing was applying a few simple biblical truths.

The disciples leveraged each other's varied spiritual gifts, talents, and abilities. They were relying on God's design, the body of Christ, to be complete. Second, they were practicing the simple truth that we are all ministers, saints. Everyone is capable and called. They not only knew they could do it, but they did it with faith and confidence. Third, they embraced the truth that there is only one God, one way, and one truth in every situation. So they relied on finding biblical, God-given direction for each situation. Sometimes God's direction was obvious. Other times, like with the refinance opportunity, these disciples had to chain several of God's principles together. But no matter the situation, they knew when they all heard the same direction, that was the direction. They wanted to follow God, and they used every talent, every team member, to find that direction. They had the right "why" for doing what they were doing. And that is the first measure of success in disciple making.

Can you imagine the simplicity of a church full of disciples like these disciples? Can you imagine no power struggles? Can you imagine not being needed to get the work done? It is possible if we succeed in making self-sustaining disciples!

How can you test your making of independent disciples? If you are an average Joe, suggest that your pastor take a four-month sabbatical. If you are a pastor, explain the experiment to your leadership team and take a four-

month sabbatical. Do not tell the church that it is an experiment. Do not set everything up for success. Do nothing to
prepare. Just go on a sabbatical. Walk away and see what
happens.

You may already know the answer: you (or your pastor)
are hopelessly needed at the church. The people are dependent on you. You are the impetus and the primary executor
of most of the work. Your staff might rally to the task, but
the people will not rally behind them picking up the ball.
Still wondering if you have succeeded in disciple making?
Ask yourself a few questions:

- *Are the average Joes ready to run? Do they know
  God's truths? Are they practicing those truths
  when no one is looking? Do they need you to
  connect the dots?*
- *If you did not teach, who would teach? What
  would be the plan? Who is capable? Who has
  already been given the experience?*
- *Do the people call you "Pastor"? Are you the
  central figure of the church, or do they see
  themselves as ministers?*
- *Are you willing to be unnecessary?*

The real question is, "Have we prepared people to live
out Christianity, to follow, on their own?" This is the one
thing that we are called to do. This is the one thing that
Jesus modeled for us. He made prepared, confident, and
skilled followers whom he released into the world. Jesus
took a sabbatical. He knew the plan would not be complete
until he left. His followers needed to rely on the Spirit of

God. The goal of discipleship is to make independent followers.

We had no choice in this experiment. My car got run off the road. But we had (and you have) a choice long before life happened. Thankfully, long before the accident, we chose to learn to succeed in disciple making. That single choice paid off when I had to be gone, but it continues to pay off every day. For the last two years, we have all embraced the success. I teach less. I write more. Jaime keeps the place together. Chandra runs the daycare. Staff meetings almost feel like a formality. God uses my years of ministry and experience to guide them through new experiences, but really, they apply his words. They are the commentary. I am just the color. And why does it work?

It works because it is God's design. God knew what He was doing. His methods worked in biblical times, and those same methods will work for you too. So often, we think that our role is to be the one, to be needed, to be necessary. But our actual role is to be like Jesus, able to leave, go to heaven or go on to the next task without the church collapsing. To successfully make disciples is to become unneeded by them.

# CHAPTER 3
# RIDDLE ME

*A ship pulls up to a dock at a wharf. The captain comes down the gangplank and onto the dock. He walks up the wharf to the boardwalk and into a restaurant. He goes in, looks at the menu, and orders a seagull sandwich. After he gets his food, he sits down in a booth and takes a bite of the sandwich. Then he pulls out his pistol and shoots himself dead. Why did he kill himself?*

I know some people do not like riddles, but I love this riddle. I use it when I speak. I use it to teach group dynamics and problem-solving. And, it always works. People love a challenge, and they dive in. But this riddle is tricky. I have seen it take hours for a group to solve, even when I give hints. People quit playing. People get mad. People think I am tricking them. When the solution is found, there are at least four responses:

- *Fist pumping and elation from those who solved it. These folks faced the challenge and beat it. They hung in there.*
- *"Why didn't I think of that?" when the light goes on in the dark room as these folks have an aha moment. These folks hung in there too.*
- *Defensiveness and justification from those frustrated, performance-oriented participants. These folks question you and the delivery. They often believe that you mislead them.*
- *"So what?" from the people who stopped playing halfway through the riddle. They got tired. Solving the riddle was not worth the effort. So they picked up their phones and checked out.*

Do you know that there are three distinct phases of learning? First, we become aware of facts (truths, if you will.) Second, we validate and reinforce those truths with other data revealing the same truth. Third, we connect those truths conceptually to other truths to discover new truths. And the cycle continues.

If you are familiar with mind mapping, you get this. Everything we learn is connected like dots connected by lines. When we think, our minds follow those lines and connections (those neural pathways and patterns) to solve problems, make decisions, and react.

Your brain is also hardwired to carry out two prime directives: survive and conserve energy. In other words, our brains are designed to protect us. Subconscious responses and quick reactions prevent us from being hit by cars, burning our hands on stoves, and much more. Our fight-orflight response to danger is an example of our brains going on autopilot to protect us. The second directive is conserving energy. We need energy to survive, and the brain consumes a lot of calories. This is why we get tired when solving complex problems. This is why our minds wander when we get bored. If there is no value in thinking, our brains lighten the load and stop working.

So what does all this have to do with measuring your success in disciple making? Think of your best-made disciple and ask the question, "How does he respond to the riddles of life?"

- *Does he think conceptually and hang in there until he solves the riddle?*
- *Does she celebrate and integrate the truths when someone else solves the riddle she could not solve?*
- *Does he challenge the answer or God Himself? Does he feel frustrated because he could not figure it out?*
- *Does she check out because it is just too tiring? Does she see the value in solving the riddle?*

We all get grumpy and tired (remember how our brains work), but overall, well-made disciples always end up in the first two categories: they solve the riddle, or they participate and celebrate the solution. Well-made disciples slow down their thinking, never letting the riddle go. They keep searching. They add truths found along the way to their arsenal of truths for extraordinary living. Well-made disciples know that each of God's truths connect to navigate the immediate unknown and, more significantly, to help them understand who God is. They also know that God will not mislead them. After all, God is in the success business. Well-made disciples expect a surprise ending where they will experience God and find a golden-nugget truth that will change their lives. Do you see the measures of your success?

The first measure of success in making a disciple is the disciple understanding the "why." In our previous examples, the why has been attached to specific truths. For example, understanding why we should tithe or why we should be selfless. In this case, the why is a broader concept. A well-made disciple knows that he does not know what he does not know. And he understands the inherent dangers of not knowing. He understands the value of enduring, meditating, learning, and listening to God as he faces the riddles of life. That value, that why, keeps him at the task, waiting on God to teach him and connect the dots.

The second measure of success in making a disciple is the disciple doing it on his own. In our previous examples, "doing it on his own" has been about the disciple doing the right thing for the right reason long after our influence fades. In this case, "doing it on his own" is about seeing the riddle and taking the challenge. It is about not giving up and not being performance oriented. Well-made disciples not only know the value of solving riddles, but they see the riddles, and they work to solve them.

The third measure of success is the disciple navigating the unknowns. In our previous examples, this has been about connecting seemingly unrelated truths to get direction and answers. In this case, it is about that and a bit more. When it comes to solving the riddles of life, well-made disciples think outside the box. They see the big picture and avoid getting bogged down in the details. The Seagull Sandwich riddle is a good example.

When it comes to solving the riddle, the seagull itself is what derails most people. They obsess over the seagull. Did the captain hate seagulls? Are seagulls poisonous? Did a seagull abuse the captain when he was a child? You cannot imagine the questions. The second distractor is the captain's current state of affairs. Was he suicidal? Did he actually die? Did someone walk into the restaurant who reminded him of a bad memory? Again, there are lots of questions. The key to solving this riddle is found in thinking about the timeline. And it takes quite a bit of time for people to get out of the details and look at the bigger picture. Even when someone asks essential questions, like, "Had he ever eaten a seagull sandwich before?" or, "Was he always a captain?" it still takes a while before participants begin to understand the solution is found in the past, not the present.

Disciples must be able to get outside the box of their immediate context. They need to be willing to challenge what they think they know. They need to integrate what they are currently learning. Well-made disciples ask a lot of questions. They answer each one, never giving up until they find the key and connect God's truths to solve the riddle. Well-made disciples rely on the Spirit to help them see the bigger picture.

Can you imagine a church full of riddle-solving disciples? These are the disciples you want leading and following before you get hit by a car. These are the disciples you want leading you!

Want to know if you have riddle-solving disciples? If you are an average Joe or emerging leader, start asking those tough, seemingly unsolvable questions. If you are a pastor or key leader, stop teaching. Do not make a big deal about it. Just stop teaching. Start asking tough questions and see what happens.

Change your midweek meeting to a game show. Ask your people things like, "What do these five biblical quotes have in common?"

*Owe nothing to anyone—except for your obligation to love one another. If you love your neighbor, you will fulfill the requirements of God's law.*
    —Romans 13:8

*Don't agree to guarantee another person's debt or put up security for someone else. If you can't pay it, even your bed will be snatched from under you.*
    —Proverbs 22:26–27

*One-tenth of the produce of the land, whether grain from the fields or fruit from the trees, belongs to the LORD and must be set apart to him as holy. If you want to buy back the LORD's tenth of the grain or fruit, you must pay its value, plus 20 percent.*
    —Leviticus 27:30–31

*If someone has enough money to live well and sees a
brother or sister in need but shows no compassion—how
can God's love be in that person?*
  —1 John 3:17


*"If you forgive those who sin against you, your heavenly
Father will forgive you. But if you refuse to forgive others,
your Father will not forgive your sins."*
  —Matthew 6:14–15


It takes a bit of conceptual thinking to figure out that
the common category is "debt." Each passage teaches us
something about owing something to others. The first three
are pretty obvious.

- *Do not be in debt to your neighbor.*
- *Do not be in debt for your neighbor.*
- *If we do not tithe, we are in debt to God. We owe
  Him something.*

The last two are a bit harder to figure out, as neither
uses the word "debt."

- *We are responsible to help our brother if we can
  help. We owe that to him.*
- *We should extend forgiveness to others. We owe
  that to them because we have been forgiven.*

Invite them to help you solve your unsolved riddles
and see how they do. Do they understand why riddle
solving is important? Do they see the riddle? Can they

solve it? How do they handle something that seems unsolvable?

One of my scripture riddles is found in Ecclesiastes. Solomon writes,

*Bread is made for laughter, and wine gladdens life, and money answers everything.*
—Ecclesiastes 10:19 (ESV)

Do you see the riddle? It is the last line that gets me. Is money the answer to everything? Was he speaking tongue-in-cheek? Money does make life simpler. But how much money does one need to give the answer? Could I live meagerly and find the answer more simply? Money cannot buy love, but money pays the bills. Right or wrong, we all know the saying "Money talks, the rest walks." It may seem silly, but there is something there that grabs me. Something deep in his words makes me think, wonder about myself, and wonder about God's provision.

When we started asking tough questions, we realized our people were not riddle solvers. Most of them had grown up in churches that were not designed to make successful, independent, riddle-solving disciples. They grew up in church systems that required leadership. The leader was the one to find the next new thing for them. The leader was the one who cast the vision for them to follow. Their churches expected them to be in Sunday school or life groups forever. And our church, apparently, was not doing much better. We wanted people to be riddle solvers like us, but our system was not designed to create riddle solvers.

Today, our disciple makers intentionally expose disciples to riddles. We ask them tough questions. In the beginning, we have to prime the pump, illustrating the value of solving tough questions. We have to push them to see the riddles in the Bible and in life. But over time, people get it. One of our favorite riddle resources is *Mystical Chapters*.[1,2] The book is a compilation of thoughts from the early church leaders as they made disciples. It is a record of their journey to understand and communicate the mysteries of God. Some of their three hundred thoughts are spot-on and thought-provoking. Other thoughts are entirely incorrect. Others are simply bizarre. We develop critical and conceptual thinking by asking disciples to confirm or deny each thought with biblical truth.

Stretching disciples to answer tough questions causes them to think conceptually. It pushes them to try to understand the heart of God and integrate His big picture into their challenges. It prepares them to become problem-solving followers of Christ, able to face and navigate the unknown. We will talk more about how you can do this in the closing chapters. For now, know that well-made disciples are riddle-solving disciples.

But riddle solving for the sake of solving riddles will only lead to arguing about myths and legends.[3] The real target is making disciples who solve riddles for the right reason: understanding God and finding truths that immediately transform their lives.

# CHAPTER 4
# SHEKEL SHACKLED

We were only into the first few weeks of discipleship when Bobbie began complaining.

"It is taking too long to get all this Bible reading done. It's killing me. I am falling behind every week unless I stay up all hours."

"What's going on? Is the reading just going slow?" I said.

"I don't think I read slowly. It's just, there is so much I want to know. And there is so much in there. By the time I read it and take notes of all my questions, I am exhausted," Bobbie replied.

Her answer did not surprise me. She was definitely caught up in the details. Whenever I asked, "What's your next highlight from the Bible?" Bobbie's answers focused on the details. Clearly, she had studied. She would tell me what others thought, what her Bible commentary said, as she referred to the context and culture of the times. Bobbie's questions were about the details. Her comments were about the details. Again and again, over and over, I would challenge her highlights and comments, asking, "How does that change your life? What truth is in that passage that you can apply?"

"Uh," Bobbie would stammer, her frustration mounting.

"It's okay. I just want you to look for useful truths. This is not Bible study. It's discipleship. The goal is to find useful truths that help you live the abundant life God wants you to live. Take another look."

It was so difficult for Bobbie. She felt like she was failing. Bobbie had been doing Bible study for years. She knew how to study. But discipleship is not about studying. Discipleship is about acquiring and applying God's truths to our lives. Being a disciple is about following God's ways, becoming like God, and experiencing a fulfilling life with Him. His ways are practical. His ways guide us. And when we get His truths, when we understand the why and do them for the right reason, those truths transform us.

We wanted Bobbie to just read the Bible, listen to her heart, and highlight truths about God. We did not want her to search for every truth. We wanted her to highlight truths that stood out in the moment. Bobbie was one of the hundreds of disciples who have walked this path in our discipleship groups. She was missing sanctification, shackled by shekels.

Jack's story is a bit different but not unique. Countless Jacks flow into discipleship groups. Jack loved to write commentary. He had so many words. So many. Jack got frustrated too. I lost count of the times I said, "Jack, I don't want to offend you in any way, but we have five guys here and only a couple hours. Can you hone down your point? What is the applicable truth? What made you go, 'Aha'?"

It was so difficult for Jack. He struggled to let go of the details even when he heard a truth. But more often than not, he was missing a forest of truth for the trees of detail. He was a scholar. But for Jack, his devil was in the details. He looked frustrated and puzzled as I asked, "Jack, when, in what situation ever, did knowing who the author of Psalms was help you make a decision, pick a life direction, or evaluate your behavior? When did the geographic location of a biblical event change how you lived? Or when did knowing the current value of a shekel help you follow God?"

But unlike Bobbie, Jack did not feel like he was failing. He felt like he was fighting to figure out what we wanted. He knew how to tear apart a passage. His notes highlighted history, language, culture, and context. Jack knew how to study. But discipleship is not about studying. It is about discovering and following God's truths for living. It is about getting to know the Father in our present context.

We wanted Jack to read the Bible, listen to the Spirit, and discover truths that stood out. We wanted him to stop justifying his process and learn to trust God's process. God longs for us to consume His applicable truths. And He promises to infuse those truths in our spirit. He promises to renew our minds as He reminds us, in real time, of those truths. We wanted Jack to build an arsenal of truths in his heart and mind. But Jack was missing the truths, needlessly notating. He was shackled by shekels.

Jack and Bobbie were not failing. They were struggling to unlearn what the church had taught them. Christian culture celebrates the details. We send our leaders off to learn Greek and Hebrew. We herald their PhDs and their detailed descriptions of biblical times. We wean new believers from topical studies to Bible studies focused on words, histories, and details. We often think, the more we know about the details of a passage, the wiser we are. And the result of this celebration of education is an endless stream of detail-oriented believers entering and leading our discipleship processes.

Granted, there are times when the details lead us to a new truth. There are times when a Greek word cannot be described with a single, simple English word. There is a time for verse-by-verse Bible study. But when it comes to following, those times are few and far between. It is far too easy to get hung up on details that have little value to transform us while missing the very truth that can transform us. Jesus gave the scholars of his day a similar warning:

*"You search the scriptures because you think that in them you have eternal life; and it is these that bear witness about me, yet you refuse to come to me that you may have life."*
—John 5:39–40 (ESV)

*"I am the way, and the truth, and the life."*
—John 14:6 (ESV)

God has made knowing Him simple. Jesus taught in a simple, understandable way. And with the Spirit of God in us, God promises that we can understand. God even promises to give us what we need when we need it. But we are deeply entrenched in the habit of studying the details.

And habits are difficult to break. In his book, *The Power of Habit*,[1] Charles Duhigg says,

> *Habits . . . emerge because the brain is constantly looking for ways to save effort. . . . When a habit emerges, the brains stops fully participating . . . . It stops working so hard, or diverts energy to other tasks. So unless you deliberately fight a habit—unless you find new routines—the pattern will unfold automatically.*

Bobbie and Jack were on autopilot. They were acting out of habit. It took time and effort to develop a new pattern of looking for applicable truth. It took energy and deliberate choice. But both Bobbie and Jack got it. Bobbie no longer focuses on shekels when it comes to following. Oh, she is still a Bible nerd and loves taking notes. But when it comes to being a disciple, Bobbie wants evident truths that she can apply. She has found the value of God's simple truths. Jack talks less and listens more, and when he speaks, everyone listens. His mind is powerful and more practical now that he focuses on clear truths that can be immediately applied to knowing God and living for God. Bobbie and Jack have shifted their discipleship focus from education to transformation. And they are thriving.

The first measure of your success is the disciple knowing the why behind the truths. Concerning shekels, success is seen as disciples sort out what matters from what has no immediate value. In essence, well-made disciples learn to work the equation backward. They begin to ask, "Why is this important?" when something pops up in the Bible or life. That simple question drives their thoughts.

That simple question filters out the unimportant, leaving only the important in its wake.

The second measure of success, doing it on his own, is seen when the disciple no longer needs to be prompted and pushed to find applicable truth. He has seen the immediate value of applicable truth, and that is his primary pursuit. The disciple is neither ignorant nor derailed by the details. He sees the details as providing illustration and support for applicable truth. His pursuit is truth, and he is confident that he will find it. The disciple relies first on God and second on commentators. It is a slight shift resulting in significant success.

The third measure of success, navigating the unknowns, can be seen as disciples stop saying, "I think," and simply state truth. Success is seen as opinion fades into the background. Success is seen as the disciple waits until he is confident of the answer. And this third measure of success is seen in the disciple's reliance on the Holy Spirit to guide his learning. He no longer believes he has to get every drop out of every word he reads. Instead, the disciple allows God to guide his heart and mind. He allows learning to become a journey instead of a race. He is looking for what God wants him to know at the moment and trusting God to remind him of the truth he needs when he needs it.

Jesus warned the scholars and leaders of his day,

> *"What sorrow awaits you teachers of religious law and you Pharisees. Hypocrites! For you are careful to tithe even the tiniest income from your herb gardens, but you ignore the more important aspects of the law—justice, mercy, and faith. You should tithe, yes, but do not neglect the more*

*important things. Blind guides! You strain your water so
you won't accidentally swallow a gnat, but you swallow a
camel!"*

   —Matthew 23:23–24


According to Jesus, the point of the scriptures is that
they reveal the source of truth and life. He is that source.
He is that truth. The details will never transform us, but
the truths of God will.

What would your church look like if the single pursuit
were applicable truth? How great would it be to have
leaders who said, "Of this, I am sure," instead of, "I think"?
What would it be like to see the chairs full of people
attracted by the transformation of others?

*You can measure your success when it comes to shekels and
notes.*

If you are making disciples, watch them. Do the disciples in your church look like followers or scholars? Do they
take endless notes while still having questions about how
to live and what to do? Well-made disciples are looking for
truths that guide them to follow God. They consume God's
Word, again and again, allowing the Holy Spirit to inspire
and teach them new truth each time. They connect God's
truths, reinforcing and expanding their understanding of
who God is and what is important to Him.

If you are not making disciples yet, watch your church's
teachers. Are your teachers full of truth, excited, and
passionate about change and transformation? Are the
members of their groups thriving in their spiritual lives? Or

are your teachers merely passing on information once a week? Disciple-making teachers are looking for spiritual progress. They elevate the application of God's truths for living above Greek, history, and theology. Well-made disciple makers are living examples of the success of following God.

If you are an average Joe, measure your church's success by what it celebrates. Does your church celebrate attendance, participation, and course completion? Do they celebrate multiplication or life change? Our church regularly steps back and looks at the disciples, the leaders, and what we are celebrating. Sometimes we do not like what we see.

A few years ago, we asked our children, teens, and adults what they were learning. The answers were dismal. The children and teens were asked, "What did you learn today?" right as they came out of their rooms. Few could remember the lesson that just ended. It got worse when we asked, "How can you use what you learn?" Our kids and teens were having fun, but applicable truth was not sticking in their hearts and minds. Even when they could remember the details of a Bible story or lesson, they had no idea what to do with it. We were not succeeding in making disciples. We were not succeeding in laying a foundation of truth for their futures. We were babysitting and entertaining while we measured attendance and fun.

With the adults, we seemed to be doing pretty well when it came to Sunday mornings. But their midweek times together showed the same results as the kids. The adults were not excited about what they were learning.

There was no passion. If they could remember what they learned, they could not identify a clear call to action.

It was time to shake things up. The people needed more value for their time invested. We needed more than fellowship. So we ditched our walk-through-the-Bible children's material. We chose simple, topical material. We created a teacher support network to reduce their preparation time. We started using introductory videos with coordinated lessons and activities. Everything was focused on delivering one verse, one applicable truth, and one take-home activity to reinforce the truth. Our goal was simple. Our strategy was biblical. We moved our kids off meat and back to milk, and everyone started thriving. Our kids can recite their verse, tell you what they learned, and know why it is important. Our teachers are passionate because they see results.

We revamped our youth programming to focus on making disciples in their context. We designed a schedule of mixed topical and Bible book studies. We used a team approach to teach, allowing the youth to hear different voices. We want them to leave with one key verse and one key truth. We reiterate and apply those truths in the monthly activities. We reinforce the truth and call the teens to action. We are moving them from milk to soft food, preparing them for meat. And it is working.

When we talked to our adults, their answers were all over the place because they were all over the place. Some people were new to the church. Some were being made disciples in our formal process. Some were well-made disciples. Each of these groups' needs, perceptions, and desires were different. Their maturities were different. But they had two things in common: they were bored to tears and saw value in their diversity. They did not want to be broken into homogenous groups. So we developed a teaching plan that provides milk, soft food, and meat on a rotating schedule. Our buffet approach uses games like Password and Hangman to introduce new truths. We study shorter, seemingly complex books of the Bible, mining them for applicable truths. We study the words of Jesus. We watch movies. And we have the people teach the people as they lead devotions and short lessons. We invested in all three areas of successful disciple making. It worked. They are having fun, they are passionate, and they are being transformed.

Overall, we retooled and reinvested in our goal of transformation and we demoted education. That focus on transformation resulted in both learning and multiplication. We began to celebrate life change instead of participation. And that celebration resulted in increased participation. Our mantra became,

*Know the truth because the truth will set you free. Find the truth. Get the why. See the value. Apply the truth. Rely on God to help you remember the truth and see how it applies right now.*

Our strategy may change over time if the people's answers change. But for now, we have released our people from the shackles of shekels. They are looking at the forest when they see the trees. People's lives are being transformed. Salvations are happening. New life is breaking out.

The questions you ask and the answers you get might

be different. Your approach, in your culture, will undoubtedly be different. But we need to remember why our people came to Christ. They came to Christ with hope for a better life, not to be educated. They came for transformation. Jesus came for the same reason. He lived, died, rose, and left so that we could return to God and be transformed. We do what we do to make followers, not scholars.

Well-made disciples long for the big picture, the big plan, and big success. They respect the details without being derailed by the details. Well-made disciples filter out what is not important to find the important. They trust the Holy Spirit to show them what God wants them to know at the moment. Success in disciple making unshackles people from shekels and leads them to sanctification.

# CHAPTER 5
# MINUS THREE, PLUS THREE

Our church recently realized that the student ministry was on autopilot. Nothing amazing was happening. No one was getting saved. Activities were, well, just blah. The teenagers were not interested, not being disciples, and not inviting friends. So we revamped it all. We got back to our roots. We figured out a simple, repeatable plan to make teenage disciples in their context. And it worked.

The student ministry grew. The teens were getting motivated. As a result, we needed more discipleship leaders. We prayed, made a list of suitable candidates, and reached out. All four of them readily accepted. Karac, a super-sharp follower, was in the first quarter of his second year of discipleship. Caleb, who had been asking to get more involved with students, was in his third year along with Kelly and Bobbie Jo. We were excited as we set the plan, advertised the new groups, and prepared the four to lead.

Teens signed up. The student ministry would add

twelve new disciples to God's Kingdom that year! Everyone was excited. Or were they? A week before the groups started, Kelly asked if she could talk. She began with an apology and then explained that she wanted to lead but did not think she could. Tears welled up in her eyes as she explained the challenges of juggling three kids, working two jobs, and being in discipleship herself. "I want to do my best in my discipleship, but the reading takes a lot of time. I don't want to give the teens less than they deserve. I am so sorry." Minus one.

The following Wednesday, only four days before the first group, Karac pulled me aside. "Got a minute?" he asked. He told a similar tale of working long hours, wanting to be a good husband and father. He also was trying to do his best in his discipleship. Then he said, "On top of it all, if I do this, I won't be taking a Sabbath. God says take a day of rest, and I get why. I need it. My family needs it. My spiritual life needs it. How can I get these kids to follow if I don't?" Minus two.

While all of this was going on, our would-have-been new missions leader quit too. Tim is a great guy. He is also a proficient leader, bright, and well loved. For several years, Tim worked hard at learning new skills to use in the field. He finished discipleship, ran projects, and excelled as a right-hand missions leader. He understood all aspects, got the job done, and made disciples while doing missions. Tim seemed to be the complete package until we put him in charge. Then it all fell apart. It collapsed. He hated leading trips. He struggled to succeed. We retrained. He invested. Again and again, it just did not work. "You know I have been praying, and I don't think I am supposed to be the guy. I am great being the guy who supports the guy. I am a great second. I think that is what God has gifted me to do. I can't lead anymore." Minus three.

Looking back at the student discipleship makeover, Caleb was excited. He prepped and was ready for the first group meeting. He had met with the student minister. He had reread *How to Make Disciples* and started doing a spiritual journal. Oddly enough, Caleb was the one we were most worried about. He travels a lot for work. He loves to go on spontaneous marathons and mega-hikes, disappearing for weeks. He was not super consistent on Sundays. He is a free spirit. But Caleb was invested in discipleship three, raised his kids well, and loved God. Caleb was consistent and serious about following God at home, at work, and everywhere else. And for two years, he had been telling us, "I really feel called to work with the teens." He has done an incredible job. He is consistent and prepared, and the teens love him. Caleb is making disciples. Plus one.

Bobbie Jo was, in our minds, another questionable pick. She is a working mom who homeschools her kids. We knew it was time for her to start making disciples and produce from the depth of her consumption. But Bobbie Jo had been saying no to us again and again as she matured in discipleship. She was trying to correct her past. For years, Bobbie Jo had said yes to everything. She found her identity in doing, her security in being a part of things. Bobbie Jo longed to be noticed. And she constantly got in over her head. She would commit to do things and never get them done. She had even quit her first discipleship group, saying, "I can't keep up." But like Caleb, this time, she said yes and showed up ready to go. Bobbie Jo is making disciples and doing a fine job of it. The teens love her. She is balancing her life, staying invested in her personal discipleship, and becoming skilled. Plus two.

Then there is Linda. As she finished up the discipleship process, she wondered if she was ready to make disciples. And she worried about time. She was finishing her post-graduate work, facing a couple of years of internship, and raising a family. In the middle of discipleship two, Linda had faced a monster hiccup in her walk and marriage—one that in most cases would have ended it all. She was broken and still working through it all at the end of her third year. Her confidence shaken, she wondered if she was worthy of making disciples. She wondered how she would do at making disciples. We wondered too. Linda was quiet. She was gentle. Could she push? Would she have the self-confidence? Fast forward to two years later, Linda is a discipleship rock star. She pushes, guides, and loves the ladies she disciples into success. She knows they can do it. Linda does her homework. She is ready for them. Linda is relentless. She readjusts, gets help, and rebalances her life when needed without ever quitting. She has seen the value, has faced the impossible, and intends to give everyone the same opportunity. Plus three.

These were six real-life scenarios. The three we thought were ready all said no. The three we wondered about all said yes. Minus three. Plus three. Our net progress was zero. Or was it?

Until now, the illustrations have measured success at the end of the game. But making disciples is a long game, and you need to measure your success all along the way. Sometimes a no is a step forward. And other times, a yes could be a step backward. You could say, "There is a time to multiply, and there is time to mature." Sometimes what seems to be a step back is a step forward. Success in making disciples is

> *how many disciples continue to follow God for the right reasons and navigate the unknowns long after your influence fades.*

Success is a long game, but you can measure your success along the way. Take Kelly's story. You can see the first measure of success, the disciple knowing the truth and the why, in her step backward. She was excited to serve God. She understood that disciples fill gaps, help with the work, and make disciples. But she also understood that she needed to take care of herself and her family. She knew that she needed to honor her commitment to her employer, working as unto God. She understood that she needed to be fully prepared for the long game of life. Kelly was drawing from a deeper well of truths. When those truths seemed to conflict, she looked at the whys, talked to God, and had the confidence to talk to her leaders. She knew that her self-worth was not on the line and was able to choose self-care. Success.

You see the same confidence in Karac's assessment. Karac's choice was made before he came to talk. He did not come for a conversation but rather a humble, clear statement of conviction. The Spirit convicted Karac that he could not disobey God. Even if he was following God's command to make disciples, he could not ignore the Sabbath. The Spirit was guiding him using a simple truth.

Karac was young and full of energy. He wanted to serve, but God was quietly protecting Karac from what he did not know. He did not know the pain and sorrow of burnout. Karac did not know his boundaries yet. What he did know was a simple truth: God designed Karac to take one day out of seven to rest. Karac did not know what he did not know, but he listened and followed. Success.

The success for Tim is found in how he faced the unknown. He was incredible at helping lead mission teams. He was a great teacher. He had patience and skill. When challenged to take the lead, he did not have to think. He chose to use his gifts to help lead others, to meet needs. But when leading missions became a mess, Tim did not quit. Instead, he started thinking. He knew that with God's help and truths, he could solve the riddle. Tim listened to the Holy Spirit. He remembered how God gives different gifts to different people. Instead of burning out, Tim found his gifts, leaned in, and helped many people succeed from the back seat. Tim was practicing discipleship on his own long after finishing a formal process. Success.

Do you see it? The success of the three that said no is not measured in what they did or did not do. Their success is found in that they followed God, along the way, in their immediate context. Caleb, Bobbie Jo, and Linda were no different. They succeeded. But not because of what they did, because of how they followed.

Caleb wanted to serve youth but waited when we asked him to wait. He kept preparing himself. Time and time again, we put him on hold. Then, when the time was right, Caleb stepped up to do the work. He sacrificed some of his "free to be me" time to follow God's call. He submitted himself to the student minister and followed well as he made followers. Success.

Bobbie Jo listened too. She knew the dangers of taking on too much. She knew her past failures. She had grown good at avoiding "doing." But she listened to her leaders' request. She stopped, prayed, and realized that this was the next checkpoint, the next step on the pathway for her. She thought well, trusted God, and adjusted her world for this next step. She was honest about her uncertainties in her ability. She leaned in. She kept adjusting. Success.

Linda questioned her ability. She did not trust herself. She did not want to shortchange the ladies she would lead. But Linda knew there was a need. She knew that she had the tools. And she trusted the Spirit of God to pull it all together. He did, and Linda is now on her second generation of making disciples who make disciples. Success.

Six different stories. Three said no. Three said yes. If you measure success based on our plans, we failed. We ended up with two discipleship groups rather than four. We were still looking for a missions leader. If you measure our success by the three success factors, we had only two successes: Tim and Linda. Only those two were at the sweet spot of success. Only those two were doing it on their own for the right reasons long after our influence faded. The other four were still being made disciples.

But if you measure our success with each disciple's success along the way, we had six successes. And that is the key to it all. Discipleship is a long game. It is a journey. You need to measure your success along the way to know that you are succeeding.

Think of it as an ultramarathon. Ultramarathons range from fifty to one hundred miles, taking up to thirty hours to complete. For most of that time, runners run alone. No crowds are lining the mountain ridges that they run on. There is no electronic tracking at the creek they cross. You can wait at the finish line to see if they succeed, but if you want to know how they are doing along the way, you need to move from checkpoint to checkpoint, cheering them on, giving them food and water. And that requires that you know where the checkpoints are.

*Measuring disciple-making success is the same. If you want to know how disciples are doing along the way, you need to know the steps that a disciple takes toward maturity.*

When our team helps folks figure out discipleship, we tell them to allow three years to make a disciple. It is like an ultramarathon, and our research and experience have taught us two things. First, "quick disciples" most often fail because they lack preparation, confidence, and skill. It takes time to remove the rocks, pull the weeds, and plow the field of a disciple's life. Second, when it takes more than three years to make a disciple, someone is not doing the work. Either the leaders are stumbling or the disciple is not investing. It is a waste of time for everyone involved.

So we allow one year (no longer) to develop each of the three success factors. We allow the time for disciples to consume, digest, and connect God's truths. We make time for disciples to practice, get out there on their own, and learn good self-care while investing in others. Our goal is long-term success for each disciple.

We have also found that there are very predictable checkpoints along the way. There is a predictable point where disciples start wanting to serve. There is a point where they want to learn to learn. There is a point where they want to get out there on their own. All in all, we have identified fourteen steps along this pathway, each occurring in a pretty predictable sequence. I explain the Predictable Pathway fully in *How to Make Disciples,* and you can find a copy of the infographic in the resource section of this book. For now, let us just put the checkpoints on top of our Venn diagram of disciple-making success.

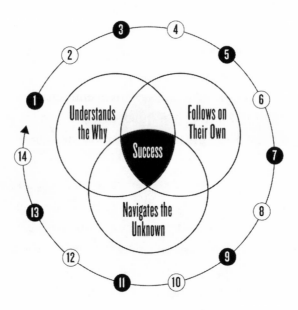

The beauty of knowing these checkpoints is threefold. First, we have a good idea of what to give each disciple at each point in their journey to get them to the next step of maturity. Second, we know what specific dangers, tests, and challenges a disciple will face at each step. Knowing the checkpoints, the steps, helps us be prepared to help disciples succeed. And third, watching for disciples to cross each checkpoint is key to measuring success along the way.

- *Kelly's next step was number ten, residency. But Kelly was pushed, tired, and needing to refuel. We needed to support that.*
- *Karac hit step nine, consecrated (all in on always following God), when he chose obedience to God's truth about resting instead of serving.*
- *Tim was well across checkpoint twelve, being servant driven, when he realized that leading missions was not the best thing for the Kingdom of God. He was Kingdom minded as he stepped across checkpoint thirteen.*
- *Caleb stepped into residency, leading while being coached, as he crossed checkpoint ten.*
- *Bobbie Jo answered the call to residency the same as Caleb.*
- *Linda crossed checkpoint eleven, leading on her own, sailed through checkpoint twelve, being servant minded, and was on to checkpoint thirteen. She was thinking about what was best for the Kingdom of God and adjusting her life.*

We use this highly predictable pathway to measure success along the way because we have observed each of these maturity steps in God's word, in the way He makes disciples. It is easy. It works. Your system might be different, but you need a plan to measure their success along the way. You need a plan to know when to push them to a yes and when a no shows both of you that the disciple is progressing in maturity. You need to know that they are moving forward.

You might ask those who are serving, "Are you fulfilled?" This incredibly vague question can start a discussion that will help you measure the health of those who are serving. Are they serving beyond their preparation? Are they burnt out? Are they doing what needs to be done or what they are designed to do? Do they know what they are designed to do? You will be amazed at the answers.

You can take a measure of your success by making a list of everyone at your church, indicating whether they are moving forward, moving backward, or stalled in the practice of their faith. If your church is larger, this will take some work. You may have to delegate the work to leaders who know the people. You might have to survey the crowd and ask them if they feel like they are moving forward. Their honest answers might shock you. Whatever it takes, you cannot measure your success until you know how the people are doing along the way.

If you are making a disciple, ask her, "Where are you in your discipleship journey?" If you have your own list of checkpoints, explain the checkpoints, and measure whether she is moving forward. Or get a copy of the Discipleship Pathway[1] and use that tool. You can measure your success by each disciple's continued success throughout his journey.

Just make sure to measure what matters. Simply measuring "doing" will not do. Success in disciple making can be found in what appears to be backward motion if that motion moves disciples to follow God more closely. You need to measure whether the disciple is doing the right things for the right reasons on their own and as they navigate the unknowns of life. You need to measure the progress of who they are. Success in the long game of disciple making is found at each step, in each choice, in each decision.

And that leads us to our final illustration of success. A success wrought with failure, denial, and pain. A success still in process. A success requiring endurance, patience, and grace. A success not for the church but for Sally.

# CHAPTER 6
# ELEPHANT

Sally was one of those people with problems. You know, the person who gets upset too quickly, takes things too personally, and seems ready for a fight. You could see there was a problem; you just did not know what was going on. She was like an open wound. Every touch resulted in a flinch of pain and shock. Sally was the person you avoided challenging. She was the person who could take a fun conversation over coffee and turn it on its head. Sally was the person most of us simply avoided. She was too much work.

When Sally began her discipleship journey, she was a hot mess. She pushed back, rationalized, and challenged every obvious truth. She was aggressive. It was clear that God's words were hitting home. However, there were great things about Sally too. She wanted a better life. She wanted to find peace, love, and stability. She believed in Jesus. Sally was serious. She was transparent. And she could handle the straight truth. When Sally was pushed, she would process and figure it out. She would talk about her challenges. But even when she pushed back, she would never run. Sally would not quit. She knew something had to change.

Sally had a whole zoo of issues, but the biggest was Elephant. A couple of months into discipleship with Barb, Sally started asking about elephants. "So I have been reading. And I have questions about other people who had elephants. I mean, some godly people had elephants. And God never said elephants were wrong."

"Well, Sally, just because they had elephants doesn't mean it was right. Why do you ask?" Barb replied.

It was then that Sally introduced Barb to Elephant. And Elephant was big. He was shocking.

"Sally, God doesn't want you to have that elephant in your life. He has a specific plan, and Elephant is not a part of that plan. Look at this verse—it says, 'No elephants.'"

"That doesn't make sense. If they could have elephants, why can't I have Elephant? I love Elephant. Elephant makes me happy," Sally said.

The conversation went on, but there was not much to say. The truth was pretty obvious. God told us not to have an elephant. It was right there in black and white. When Sally's leader came to us for help, we reminded her,

- *We are not their therapists.*
- *We are not their priests.*
- *We are not their accountability partners.*
- *Ask her, "What does the Bible say about it?"*
- *Ask her, "What are you going to do about it?"*

Barb asked. Sally's answer was shocking. "I am not going to do anything about it. David had an elephant. Why can't I?" Barb did her best to help Sally see God's truths and understand the whys behind God's ban on elephants. Sally listened but was not convinced.

Barb kept discipling, and Sally kept coming to discipleship. She learned truths. She applied truths. But Elephant was always in the room. Could Sally be a well-made disciple if she refused to accept and apply God's truths to her elephant?

Along the way, I wondered if I should do something about this whole elephant stuff. Was it my business? What is the role of a church leader? How far did I reach? Should I confront her for her own good? What if the disease spread? I did not know what to do, so I did nothing but pray and wait.

In the following year of discipleship, Sally ended up in my coed group of nine. We started reading the Bible cover to cover, and when we hit the parts about elephants, Sally asked, "How can it be wrong to have an elephant if godly men like David had elephants? God never said David was wrong."

"Sally, godly people can do wrong things. Elephants did not work out well for David or anyone else. Look at all the examples in the Bible. Just because something is recorded in the Bible does not mean it was good. Sometimes stories are just historical records."

I pointed out David's regrets. Then I asked, "Why is this an issue for you?"[1]

"Well I want to be up-front with you. You are discipling me," Sally said.

And then she introduced me to Elephant. Even though I knew about it, her detail and explanation still shocked me. It became a reality. The idea that someone would have an elephant was foreign to me. This was new territory for me, the unknown. All kinds of questions flooded in. Should I get my wife to meet with both of us? Could I talk to her alone? What's my exposure here? I had no idea what to do.

There was much conversation, much explanation of God's truths, and a ton of denial. I reiterated that just because David had an elephant did not mean that elephants were right. I asked her what truths she had learned about elephants. I pressed her to think it through. Our conversation ended with this thought:

"Sally, the thing I care most about is you. If God's truths say, 'Do not,' and you keep doing, you will not be following Him. More than anything, I want you to follow Him. Not only in this area but in every area."

I called her to the truth. I called her to apply the truth. I accepted her as she was. I trusted God with her. And I left it alone.

Several weeks later, as we covered the Bible verses people had highlighted, Sally had the oddest look on her face.

"Sally, what's up?"

"I'm Jezebel," she said.

The room got quiet. I said nothing. The air was thick. Right there in front of everyone, Sally said, "I am that controlling woman leading Sam astray. I am that woman taking his strength and manipulating."

It stayed quiet, and I let the moment sink in.

"Well now you know what you need to do, right?"

"Repent?" she offered.

"Yep. Okay, next highlight. Who has the next highlight?"

Sally's face remained pensive. Our group went on to cover the next aha moment from the Bible reading. We were not teaching about Jezebel. Sally had not highlighted Jezebel as she read that week. Someone else had highlighted Jezebel. Sally was feeding off the crumbs of someone else's aha moment when it happened. God took someone else's question and turned it into a catalyst that began to change the very core of "who Sally was."

I had to work to control my excitement. This was a big moment. God was working in Sally. The Holy Spirit was convicting her. If God could reach her at this level, this could be the beginning of the end for Elephant! But it was not. Sally kept Elephant. She loved him. Elephant made her happy.

Later that year, Sally's husband and I were on a mission trip when God prompted me to do something terribly uncomfortable.

"Sam, you're in discipleship. I mean, you're all in. Can I ask you a question?"

"Sure," he replied. "Is something wrong?"

"Well, I, uh, don't want to get in your pie, but I was wondering about Elephant."

Sam stopped in his tracks. "Sally told you about him?"

"Yes."

"I hate this," Sam said.

"I get it. I can't imagine how I would feel."

Tears welled up and spilled over as he replied, "It sucks.

I was done with elephants after I got into discipleship. I asked her to get rid of Elephant, to kick him out of her heart, but she won't. And I don't want to lose her."

Our conversation ended with a prayer and me pushing him to share his feelings with Sally. Our friendship got deeper and our discipleship more genuine. I was beginning to really hate Elephant.

Fast forward another year, Sally was in discipleship two with a new leader. It was a female group. A few months in, they were reading about elephants, and it came up again. Yes, again! The same questions, challenges, and justifications. Jenny, Sally's new leader, reached out. I gave the same advice. Push Sally to face God's truths. Push her to decide whether she would follow. Emphasize the bigger picture. What was interesting was that Sally was following and progressing in almost every other area of her life. She would see the truth, apply the truth, and reap the benefits of following God. But this one big Elephant still remained. It made no sense.

Sam was in my discipleship group that year. Week after week, Sam would pray that God would show him what to do with his marriage. I kept asking, "What is your role as a partner? What is your role as a fellow Christian? When do you draw the line and say, 'It's time for a change'?"

Throughout the year, I had no idea of what Sam and Sally decided to do about Elephant. They never brought it up. God did not tell me to bring it up again. I stayed quiet. Jenny stayed quiet. We all kept praying.

The year of discipleship ended. Sam had finished the process and signed up to lead a group of guys through discipleship one. Sally told me that she was going to take a year off formal discipleship.

"I need a break," she said.

"Why?"

"I think I need to pause and work on myself."

"Pause what? The formal process or following God?" I asked.

"Well of course I am not going to stop following God."

"So you have a plan? I mean, what will you do with the time you were investing in learning His truths?"

Unlike most people who take a break, Sally was not checking out. She was convinced God wanted her to take a year off. Sally was following God. And she had a plan.

"I am going to read the Bible cover to cover on my own, I was going to ask for some good books to read, and I am going to lean in on my relationship with Sam and the kids." And she did.

Sam and Sally got into marriage counseling. It turns out Sally was not well loved as a child and had a huge hole and a lot of trauma in her heart. And Sally was so serious about it that she almost lost her job when she refused to miss a counseling appointment for a work emergency. Sally read her Bible, and other helpful books, and poured into her kids like never before. Love was winning, and most of the cages in Sally's zoo were empty now.

I was so excited when I heard that Sam had drawn a line in the sand, shared his love for her, and told her it was time for Elephant to go. Finally, the largest cage in Sally's life was empty! Discipleship was working. Or so I thought until I sent the rough draft of this chapter for Sally to review. I was so disillusioned as I read her email.

*Although the first part is hard to read, I believe it is probably correct. I was broken, hard to get along with, and it was probably easier for most people to just avoid me. It wasn't until I started discipleship that I felt a true connection with God. Before, I was just going through the motions of being a Christian without the Spirit leading me. Taking this year off of discipleship, I have discovered that I want to chase after God, and I have. I feel like I have a relationship now with Him without boundaries. I have bad days, but through counseling and prayer, I now know there is nothing that I can't overcome with God. I do feel like I am succeeding in following God. I know I must rely on Him and Him alone. I have changed over the last few years, primarily because of discipleship and learning to chase after God.*

*But you can't use this story because Elephant is still part of my life. I know you love us, and this news will hurt at first, just like what I read in the chapter hurt me at first. I know this is not what you wanted to hear, but I hope you will continue to accept me.*

If you are thinking, "This isn't reading much like a success story," then you are feeling what I was feeling. I wanted to throw up my hands and quit everything. I am sure you understand. It is such a terrible feeling to think you are succeeding at your life call and then find out you might not be. It is easy to get angry. Angry at the enemy. Angry at all the hours that seem wasted. It is also easy to ditch the Sallys of our lives, to quit them. After all, why cast our pearls before swine? Why keep investing if people will not get rid of their elephants?

Granted, there is a time to stop investing. There is a time when we must call people to repentance before they can move forward in discipleship.[2] But our decisions need to be driven by God and approved by God. Our feelings need to be based on truth.

Elephant might be ugly and shocking, but in every other area, Sally was working and applying truth. She was still consuming God's truths. She understood the whys and was following on her own. Sally's life was being transformed. Her success could be measured as we observed her passing checkpoint after checkpoint in spiritual maturity. Even while justifying and pushing against the truth, she was still fighting to understand, reconcile, and find her way. Isn't that success?

The last illustration, "Minus Three, Plus Three," introduced the idea that you need to measure your success along the way. Sally's story reinforces that idea, adding another vital concept. Your success cannot be measured by any single transformation at any single point in time. The disciple is not failing as long as she is engaged.

You know this. Some things take more time than others. Some transformations come on the heels of many other transformations. There are times when God lays a foundation for a coming change. Disciple makers need to listen to God, use His plan and His timing. There is a time to push. There is a time to invest and wait quietly. As long as they are moving toward Him and after Him, they are succeeding. You are succeeding.

Can you imagine a place where sinners are accepted despite their sin? How many people can we rescue if we are willing to love, accept, and endure with them as they work through their issues? How many people will hang in there if we help them see their measurable success along the way?

Sally knows she is succeeding. She can measure her success by the checkpoints she has passed. Now Sally stands at checkpoint nine, consecration.[3] She seems to know that Elephant is not good for her, that he is wrong. Whether or not Sally will go all in, following God no matter what, remains to be seen.

Our success to this point came through God-directed patience and continued investment. None of Sally's leaders felt it was time to disconnect or ask her to leave the group. We were heartbroken but hopeful. We believed in the power of God's truth and Spirit to convince Sally, but we had no idea what to do. We wanted Sally to ditch Elephant. We wanted her to have the abundant life that God desired for her. We kept discipling. Sally kept growing. Her success along the way was our success.

But Elephant is still standing in the room. He is still shocking. We still want her to stop, but our job is to make a follower of God, not someone acceptable to us. To do that, we need to follow God. We need to continue to speak when He says, "Speak." We need to wait when God says, "Wait." We need to follow Him step by step whether or not we understood His complete plan. Through us, God can show her His confidence, endurance, and hope for her best day. There may be more things to heal before Sally conquers this one symptom. There may be other truths that Sally needs to work through before she can connect the dots on what seems evident to all of us. Our success will only be found in patient, continued investment as we follow God.[4]

Not every disciple will have a big sin to conquer. Not every disciple will have to work through many truths to apply one truth. But God has a specific plan for each person. We need to be listening to that plan. Pushing when He says, "Push." Waiting uncomfortably when He says, "Wait." Success in the long game of making a disciple requires that we believe in God and His disciple.

Are you succeeding in the uncomfortable and seemingly impossible? If your church is a place where honesty and transparency are rewarded, you are on your way. If you are willing to say that sin is sin without condemning the sinner, you are on the right path.

When it comes to messy Sallys, you can measure your success by asking a few questions.

- *How much do I know about those I am making disciples?*
- *Do I talk to God about how to make each disciple?*
- *Am I asking God what to do and when to do it?*
- *Am I more interested in who they can become and are becoming or their current behavior?*
- *Do I have the patience of Christ?*
- *Are disciples progressing in other areas even though "one thing" does not seem to be getting fixed?*

The world is full of messy Sally's who will struggle. If we are to succeed in discipleship, we need to walk with them along the way. We need to help them see God's truths and understand the whys behind those truths. We need to cheer them on to do it on their own. And we need to patiently guide them as they conquer their unknowns. We need to stay in the game as long as God is in the game.

Making disciples is God's journey with each and every disciple. He is the one who transforms them into followers. He is the one who makes disciples. And God has one simple way of making people who continue to follow Him for the right reasons and navigate the unknowns long after our influence fades. The following chapters talk about how we can get people there—God's way.

# CHAPTER 7

# PREPARED

UNDERSTANDING THE WHY

I spent years trying to make disciples with little long-term success until I studied discipleship in the Bible. I found something amazing when I looked at how God made followers—God has one very simple way of making disciples. You see it in the Old Testament, and you see it in the New Testament. All throughout the Bible, God uses one method to successfully make disciples. First, he prepares them, then he builds their confidence, and then he helps them become skilled at following him in every situation.[1] You can see this in the way Jesus made disciples.

- *Jesus prepared them by calling them to surrender, teaching them truth, and asking them questions to help them get the why.*
- *Then He built their confidence by testing them with more questions. He put them in situations where they had to do it with His guidance—like we do with medical residents.*

- *Then He released them to do it on their own. He released them to live, to lead, and to make disciples. He released them to be the light to the world. And they did a pretty good job.*

My favorite definition of a disciple (the one I teach and use) helps me measure my success in disciple making. Not only is it simple and repeatable, but it also clarifies the making of disciples for me.

*Making disciples introduces people to God, who loves and understands them, helps them understand who they are and what they can be, helps them apply God's transforming truths, and releases them as prepared, confident, and skilled to live their best life ever on earth.*[2]

A well-made disciple is prepared, confident, and skilled at following God. If we put that definition on top of our Venn diagram, it looks like this.

Step one will always be preparing them, and Jesus's method of preparing them reflects what we know as the Socratic method. Michelle Fabio explains the Socratic method this way:

> *Socrates sought to expose contradictions in the students'*
> *thoughts and ideas to then guide them to solid, tenable*
> *conclusions. . . . The principle underlying the Socratic*
> *method is that students learn through the use of critical*
> *thinking, reasoning, and logic. This technique involves*
> *finding holes in their own theories and then patching*
> *them up.*[3]

We do not have a record of everything Jesus said to His disciples or every way He taught them truth. But it is interesting to see what His disciples thought was important. Their historical record reflects Jesus using parables, asking questions, and answering questions with questions. He challenged His followers to understand the bigger picture, the "why" of God, and His truth. He made them put it all together. And when they asked, "Why do you speak in riddles?" Jesus responded, "So that only those who have the Spirit will understand."[4] Without God, without His Spirit, there is no understanding.

Jesus created what I call "thought vacuums." He created time and space for the disciples to think through the truths. He pushed them to understand why these truths were important to God. Jesus not only exposed them to truths, but through the why, He exposed them to the character of God. In so doing, He created the opportunity for people to understand what was important to their Creator.

The value of God's commands became clearer. The way God's truths come together for successful living became more and more evident. His disciples were no longer following the miracles. Instead, they longed to be like the miracle maker. The value of getting disciples to think through discreet truths and discover truths in God's words should not be underestimated. But this type of learning is not the norm in our churches and Bible studies.

Most of our church systems keep people dependent on leaders to disseminate truth. Most discipleship pathways, processes, and materials are no different. There is no plan for graduation or releasing the disciples to succeed on their own. The church gives little chunks of information that can be easily digested. On one end of the spectrum, we give them topical studies on how to handle money, sex, marriage, anger, loss, and the like. On the other end of the spectrum, we give them historical, theological, and Greek definitions. They study and study and study but experience little personal transformation. Indeed, there is nothing wrong with topical learning, and understanding history can help us unravel the riddle of a complex biblical statement by putting it in context. It is just that these methods of teaching often become the end instead of the means. Topical (or relevant) teaching becomes the milk that we dole out. We address the hot topics. We answer immediate questions. We avoid tricky topics like Jesus saying that God allowed divorce. And we leave disciples hopelessly unprepared to face what they do not know yet. They must always return to the master teachers within our walls. Historical and factual teaching often degrades into education instead of leading to transformation. Disciples understand the three Greek words for love without being transformed by those truths. They feel complete knowing all the details but, as Jesus said,

> *"Hypocrites! For you are careful to tithe even the tiniest income from your herb gardens but you ignore the more important aspects of the law—justice, mercy, and faith. You should tithe, yes, but do not neglect the more important things."*
>
> —Matthew 23:23

The solution to successfully making disciples requires what Dan Heath describes as an upstream solution.[5] Instead of heroically helping followers with the immediate problem, we need to prepare them for their future. We need to expose them to truths long before they need them. And we need to make sure they understand why those truths are essential to their success. We can teach the data (the truths), but they will never get (or own) the why unless we create thought vacuums. Disciples need to think through God's truths and listen as His Spirit works within them, pulling it all together. Deep thought and meditation on God's truths are nothing new. The saints of God have been practicing this type of learning for centuries. We are encouraged to meditate on God's words,[6] think about His words, get the truth, and understand God through His truths. Jesus's parables, frustrating questions, and tricky answers created thought vacuums. Jesus created ambiguity as He exposed people to the truths of God. That ambiguity caused them not only to think but, in the long run, to succeed.

Eugene Peterson, best known as the author of *The Message Bible*, once said,

> *There is a way we can preach without being bullies, or being in a hurry . . . and without having everything tied down. I think sermons suffer greatly for a lack of ambiguity.*

Think about it. What has made you a success at knowing, understanding, and synthesizing God's truths? I will bet (and I hope) it is that you know His truths. You have read the Bible cover to cover many times, digesting and assimilating the truths of God. You have a complete picture of God's love, design, desires, and intentions. You have sorted out the uncommon and challenging. You have faced the seemingly cruel wars that God commanded by understanding that he was defending his children. You see that those physical wars are only a picture of the spiritual warfare in high places that continues to this day. You get God. You know the value in His truths. You have tested and applied those truths no matter how illogical they seem. You are thankful, grateful, and wholly dependent on God. You have learned to listen to the Holy Spirit. You have fallen and gotten back on the horse. If you have found success as a disciple, no doubt your success started with being exposed to God's truths. And your success grew exponentially as you understood more of the whys.

If you want your disciple to understand the why of applying God's truths to his life, you must first expose him to all of God's truth. You need to ditch the resources and get him to read God's word, cover to cover. The Bible is the upstream resource, the magnum opus of God. Instead of having them read topical and historical study guides, walk with them through the Bible. I know. It sounds too old school, and many will say, "People won't read the Bible cover to cover. It is too much to ask." But disciples will read it if they see the value in your life. And they will keep reading it as they find its significance in their lives.

As you walk through the Bible with them, I encourage you to make sure it does not become a performance trap. I encourage you not to teach, not to lecture. Do not let them focus on shekels and notes. And do not let them read study notes from anyone else. Just get them to read God's words. Remind them that there must be something important in there for God to have it all written down. Teach them to expect to find something when they read. Encourage them not to write endless notes that distract their minds from hearing what God is saying in their hearts. Push them to read a little each day. Have them highlight the things that amaze them[7] and useful truths they can apply to daily living.

Let them read it on their own, and when you get together, stay out of the way. Let the Holy Spirit do the work in their hearts. Do not talk about what you see. Listen to what they see. Prompt now and then. Maybe even expose them to a truth they missed here and there. But mostly, stay out of the way. Create thought vacuums for them by answering questions with questions. Let them try to figure out the why of God's truths. Ask them again and again, "Why is that important? How will it transform your life? Where else does that truth apply?"

To a great extent, you will have to deprogram them

from the very systems we have created. You will have to challenge them to think on their own (well, actually with the Holy Spirit!). It may seem ludicrously simple, but they need His words, not our words. They need His Spirit, not our mentoring. They need His "why," not our constant teaching.

You succeed in making a disciple when they get the why, when they do it on their own, and when they are successful at making decisions when there is no discreet direction in God's Word. Your first measure of success is found in the disciple understanding the why. Your second measure of success is found when they do it on their own, for the right reasons.

# CHAPTER 8
# CONFIDENT

## DOING IT ON THEIR OWN

Jordan's first six weeks at Belmont University were tough. I will never forget the late-night phone calls made from the stairwell outside her dorm room. Jordan had never shared a room, and she was frustrated with her roommates. One was just there, never interacting. The other was nice but culturally different. Jordan was missing her boyfriend and learning to trust him. The list of new challenges grew as she adjusted to life on her own in a whole new world. We would pray and talk, and I would give what felt like useless, hopeless encouragement and ideas. More than anything in the world, I wanted to get in my car, drive to Nashville, and just hold her. Those first six weeks were tough; hanging up the phone was horrible. But week seven came without a phone call. Week eight's family visit went well. Jordan was so excited as she showed us the campus. The calls came farther apart until, one day, I realized I had not talked to her in weeks.

Jordan was surviving the challenges and thriving in her new world. She sorted out the good friends from the, well, not so good. She tested churches until she picked one all on her own. Jordan kept her faith and took a few left turns, but she figured it all out. Now and then, she would call when something new and puzzling happened, picking up a bit of advice. Jordan was growing into an independent woman. And our relationship changed.

Jordan and I were the talkers in the family. We would talk and talk about everything. I'll never forget the day she explained, "Dad, sometimes I don't call because you ask so many questions. Like, way too many questions." So began my era of learning to throttle my longing to know everything and, instead, let her share what she wanted. Then there was the time she said, "Can you just listen and not give me a ton of advice or Bible?" She sounded like my wife! Those adjustments took time. Each was difficult. Still, I am glad I actually listened to Jordan—and listened to other wise people.

One of those people was the Dean of Something or Other who spoke at Jordan's matriculation into college. Jordan was sitting somewhere down on the floor with a couple thousand freshmen. I was sitting high in the stands, scanning to find my girl, when he began talking. The dean warned us not to be helicopter parents—hovering around trying to protect our kids but often preventing their natural development. He reassured us that the faculty and staff were pretty good at guiding freshmen. He told us about the university programs designed to help them adjust to their new lives. He encouraged us to do our best to stay out of the way, to wait for calls instead of calling. He urged us not to make it about us and to trust the process. His words were the words that kept me at home when Jordan called late at night, crying. His words were some of the words that helped me process Jordan's growing independence.

It was difficult to let go, not to worry. I trusted Jordan, but I did not trust the world. There was so much that she did not know. Worse, she did not know that she did not know. But without a doubt, the gravest challenge was accepting that I was not "Daddy" anymore. I was not the foundation, the safety net, or the one she would talk to first. I was no longer the guy who rode in on a white horse when things got tough. If Jordan was going to make it in life, she had to do it on her own. It was time. She knew the "whys" behind the incredible truths we had worked through as she grew up. If I had done my job well, if God was God, Jordan could get it. She could figure it out.

And she did. She made some mistakes, but she made more successes. And she did most of it on her own or with her new friends and advisors. Our relationship changed. Jordan is still my daughter, but she is a woman. We talk more like peers now about the usual stuff. She asks for thoughts when her family faces new challenges, but she does life on her own. I am confident in Jordan. She is confident. And I generally stay out of her way.

Discipleship is like this. There needs to come a time to drop disciples off at college. You can sit by the phone. You can be ready. But you need to sell the helicopter. You need to plan to let them go long before the time comes. And when the time comes, you need to accept your new role, trust them, trust your work preparing them, and help them become more and more confident. From the beginning of making a disciple, your role is to get him to confidently follow God—not you. Your discipleship plan must point toward independence from you and interdependence with God. Every step along the way, you should be working toward your unemployment. That is the long game of success in making disciples.

*Your success in disciple making will be measured by how many disciples continue to follow God for the right reasons and navigate the unknowns long after your influence fades.*

Do you remember the keys to my favorite definition of discipleship?

- *Introduce them to God, who loves and understands them.*
- *Help them understand who they are and what they can be.*
- *Help them apply God's transforming truths.*
- *Release them.*

There should be a time when your influence fades. You need to have a plan to make that happen, and when it happens, you need to embrace your new role. Enjoy your new relationship, admire the disciple's success, and move on. Go make another disciple. Follow the plan that God and Jesus laid out for us.

With that said, there is work for you to do as they move from preparation to confidence. Mother eagles know when it is time for their eaglets to learn to fly. But they instinctively know that learning to fly is a process. The mother will push her eaglet out of the nest so it can learn to fly.

She will follow it as it falls, catching it at the last minute and repeating the process again and again. Building a disciple's confidence is like you teaching and them learning to fly. You do not want to kick them out of the nest too early, but you need to kick them out of the nest so they will continue to mature. And when it is time for him to fly, you need to be ready to catch him while his wings develop. It takes time.

Do you remember my favorite riddle about the captain and the seagull sandwich? There is something to learn about humans within riddle solving. Humans are fiercely independent. They want to win. They want to figure it out on their own. Children are a window into this world. They long to do "it" on their own. They want to feed themselves. They want to go out on their own. Teenagers reflect this desire as they try to live life on their own, testing the boundaries of every truth you have taught. They want to get it themselves. The desire for independence, the desire to figure it out, is inherent in our nature.

You see this when people hang in there and solve the riddle. You also see it in the people who fight against the riddle makers and riddle leaders. Both are confident (right or wrong) in their riddle-solving abilities. But there is another category of people when it comes to riddles: the people who never even start the riddle-solving process. They are not confident when it comes to riddles. They say things like, "I am just not good at stuff like this," and, "It's too hard. I'll never figure it out."

Erica was this person.[1] Our discipleship group was reading *The Art of War*. Each week, they would read, and we would discuss Sun Tzu's warfare strategies, connecting them to the topic of spiritual warfare. You could hear her sigh each time we opened his book. Her body language screamed insecurity. You could watch her shift from engaged to disconnected. She hated it. She thought that she could not connect Sun Tzu's warfare strategies to biblical truths about spiritual warfare. "My brain doesn't work this way. I just stare at the pages. I can't see how this connects," she said. But that was not the problem. Erica was brilliant, and she knew how to connect the dots of God's truths. She had proven it again and again. The real problem was that Erica did not believe in herself. She did not think she could handle this new challenge in critical thinking. I had pushed the group out of the nest with this exercise. Now, my role was to show Erica that she could connect the dots. I needed to move her beyond the frustration of watching other group members get it. I needed to show her how to trust herself and the Spirit. I needed to help her learn, step by step, to fly in this new realm.

Your role in helping make confident followers of God is twofold: have a plan to push them out of the nest and help them manage their level of confidence. How do you help them manage their level of confidence so that they will succeed?

- *You throttle the ones who are already confident. You do your best to keep them in the nest until they are ready to learn to fly. You teach them to slow down, to wait on God, and to check their preparedness.*
- *You help the defiantly confident to find humility so that they will succeed. You guide them out of*

*arrogance, ignorance, and insecurity to a place where they listen and value the words of God and others. You teach them the beauty of surrendering and letting God help.*

- *You encourage those who are not confident. You show them that they are designed to fly. You model flying for them. You cheer them on through success and failure. You never give up, and you never let them give up because you know God's plan is for them to be independent, self-sustaining followers.*

Eugene Peterson paraphrases Paul's words related to our self-confidence in *The Message:*[2]

*Take a good look, friends, at who you were when you got called into this life. I don't see many of "the brightest and the best" among you, not many influential, not many from high-society families. Isn't it obvious that God deliberately chose men and women that the culture overlooks and exploits and abuses, chose these "nobodies" to expose the hollow pretensions of the "somebodies"?*

—from 1 Corinthians 1:26–28

Paul's observations bring hope to those who are not confident. God rarely chose the brightest and the best. He chose nobodies. Think about it. Moses could not speak well. Paul stuttered. Abraham gave his wife to another man. David was little. Peter was a fisherman. None of the disciples went to seminary. The list goes on and on.

As Paul continues, his words expand to address the already confident and the defiantly confident.

> *[God did this so that no one can brag in his presence.]*
> *[30]And because of him you are in Christ Jesus, who became to us wisdom from God, righteousness and sanctification and redemption, [31]so that, as it is written, "Let the one who boasts, boast in the Lord."*
> —1 Corinthians 1:29–31 (ESV)

Do you see it? All our ability comes from God. In comparison to the world, most of us are nobodies. In comparison to God, we are all nobodies. But with God, we can all become somebody, people who follow God with confidence. The second measure of success in disciple making is people doing it on their own, for the right reasons. And that requires confidence in God's truths and in our ability to succeed.

Well-seasoned confidence comes from knowing and doing. When it comes to knowing, the more we know, the more confidence we have. When we see an applicable truth once, we have direction. When we see that same truth illustrated many times in different passages, our confidence in that truth grows. We begin to see the bigger picture of God's desire for us. We begin to understand the importance and nuances of that truth. Our confidence in God's truth then builds our confidence in direction and decision-making because we see and understand the same truth again and again. We become convinced, confident, of the correct direction.

In the same way, repeated success in doing builds confidence in practicing discipleship. Erica is a good example here. She had a slow start at connecting God's truths to Sun Tzu's warfare truths. But with each connection she made, she grew more confident in her ability to synthesize God's truths into how she understood the world around her.

Confidence in God's truths and our abilities leads to independence, doing it on our own. That confidence is always built upon preparation and practice. This is where your second task comes into play. If you want your disciple to "do it on their own," you need to have a plan to get them doing it on their own. And you need that plan long before you make your first disciple. How do you do that? You have three key opportunities:

- *Listen to their questions and frustrations;*
- *Listen to their prayers; and*
- *Push them into new opportunities.*

Listen to the challenges and decisions facing the disciple. Listening opens the door to help him build his confidence in God's truths. As you listen, hold your answers, thoughts, and advice even if you know the correct path. Instead, ask, "Is there a verse or truth about this?" When disciples come up with a truth, ask, "Where else does God talk about this?" Keep going until they run out of useful truths. Trust them to listen to God and find the answer. Trust the Spirit to show them multiple instances of the same truth. You may need to prime the pump now and then, but never forget the power of thought vacuums. Listen to them. Guide them to God's repeated answers, and you will see their confidence and independence grow.

Listen to their prayers. Stop them when they pray for an answer that they already know. Just interrupt them and ask, "Didn't God already provide that answer?" When they pray for guidance, ask them later, "Who in the Bible faced this same challenge? How did they handle it? Did God give them direction?" Help them think about what they already know. Help them see how what they know applies in their life. Help them stack up truths that convince them of the right path and choices. Take them off autopilot and help them learn to fly.

Have a plan to push them out of the nest. This may be your greatest challenge. But pick out an island to drop them on, cut the strings, and push them into things that stretch them to do it on their own. Kick them out of the nest while cheering them on the entire time, "You got this. You are prepared. Trust the Spirit." Challenge them to go on a mission trip, take a teaching role, speak on a Sunday, or make a disciple themselves. Think ahead and all along the way. Make a plan to push them out of the nest. Our church does all these things with intentionality.

Each disciple maker has a calendar of new challenges for every disciple they make. They develop a rough plan of "pushes" long before they even begin making a disciple. Our most significant push is asking the disciple to make a disciple before they start their third year of discipleship. It is a big push. The disciples rarely feel ready and confident. And we spend quite a bit of time catching them before they crash into the ground. But they gain confidence. They figure it out, and the results are incredible. Disciples who have made disciples enter year three with more attentiveness, insight, and confidence than those who have not.

Look for opportunities to get them doing it on their own. Be ready to rescue them as you live life on the edge together. Then cut the strings and let them be real boys and girls.

Being transformed, doing it on their own, brings glory to God and success to the followers. And when they succeed, you succeed. Have confidence in what you have done and in who they are becoming. Trust them. Help them become independent, self-sustaining disciples. Your second measure of success is your disciple doing it on his own for the right reasons. The third measure is found when he navigates the unknown.

# CHAPTER 9
# SKILLED
## FACING THE UNKNOWN

For four years (yes, four years), I have been putting a 1956 Thunderbird back together. This "gift" from a dear friend and mentor, Doc, arrived at my house in boxes. A friend of his disassembled it and then decided not to become a classic car restorer. Now it was mine. There was a box of old, worn hoses. There was a box of rusty, oily nuts, bolts, screws, and washers—none of them matched up, and there was no sign where they went. Boxes of water pumps, alternators, gadgets, and brackets took over my garage.

Not one to shrink from a challenge, I joined Thunderbird forums, ordered manuals, and began to sort out the parts. I recruited a few friends who knew more than I did about engines. I studied, asked a ton of questions, and four years later, I was ready to turn the key. Everyone assembled in the driveway. We hooked up the battery and turned her over, and over, and over. We adjusted the ignition, primed the carburetor, and tried again, and again, and again. She would almost fire up, and then she would quit. Exhausted and beyond our scope of knowledge, we quit too.

Enter Bedford. Bedford is known locally as an expert with automobiles and engines. He retired from the automobile service industry as a service manager, having worked his way up from a basic mechanic. Bedford loves cars. He has experience with old cars and new cars. He can handle both foreign and domestic automobiles. Bedford has worked on almost every type of vehicle, from restoration to repairs. He has even built race cars from the ground up. Bedford understands all the systems—brakes, ignition, suspension, electrical, and so on. He is skilled at auto repair and maintenance. And Bedford knew how to get the T-Bird running. He saw the problems and knew how to fix them. Bedford has skills that make the unknown known.

Interestingly, Bedford has never worked at an auto manufacturing plant. He has never designed an engine. He has never assembled a new car. He has never worked the line. Instead, Bedford has learned how cars work. He has learned the systems of cars. He has worked on real car problems. Bedford's skill comes from his exposure to automobile truths and his ability to synthesize those truths into solutions.

And that is the difference between Bedford and an auto manufacturing line worker. We would never say that a line worker who mastered one station, one task, was skilled at automobiles. If he learned every assembly job in the plant, we might call him skilled with that car. But we would never call him skilled at automobiles. He is only assembling cars—on top of that, only one model. He is following clear, known truths about putting together a single automobile. He knows little of how brakes work, how to fix a faulty valve, and the list goes on.

There is a time for a focused skill like assembling the block of a new car. If you get cancer, you want someone who is an expert in your cancer. If you are selling a house, you want an expert in the field. The list goes on. But life is not that specific. Life is messy. It is full of the unknown and unexpected. If life is an automobile, you want to be Bedford. And you want the disciple you make to be Bedford.

The third measure of your disciple-making success is the ability of the disciple to navigate the unknowns of life. When there is no clear biblical answer, he can figure it out. He can conceptualize and synthesize seemingly unrelated truths and principles. He can tie those truths together to diagnose what is wrong and to do what is right. He can evaluate his circumstances and make great decisions.

Most of our modern church systems pump out auto assembly-line workers. We are pretty good at producing people who will follow clear instructions in the specific stations of life. We talk about marriage, family, ministry, and work, giving some great answers. We educate people about biblical doctrines and principles. We even indoctrinate and assimilate people into our specific methods and denominational beliefs. But we are not as good at creating independent people who can navigate the unknowns of life without our help. We are trying to get paint-by-the-number followers to create a Picasso. And more than often, they are left guessing when it comes to the unknowns of life.

Sin is an excellent illustration of the need for disciples to successfully face the unknown. There are three ways to sin. You can do a don't. You can not do a do.[1] And you can do a doubt. The first two types of sin are quickly dealt with as you learn God's useful truths about living life on this earth. You can see his "do not" truths. You can see his "do" truths. You can learn the value (the why) of these truths as you see them reiterated again and again. But the third type of sin, doing a doubt, is a bit more vague. Paul wrote the people of Rome about it.

> *But whoever has doubts is condemned if he eats, because the eating is not from faith. For whatever does not proceed from faith is sin.*
> —Romans 14:23 (ESV)

Do you see it? Paul was addressing a gray area of doing —eating meat sacrificed to idols. He argues that we are free to eat the meat, but he also argues that we should not eat it if eating it hinders the cause of Christ. Then he wraps up his argument in the first half of verse twenty-three, essentially by saying,

> *But whoever has doubts is condemned if he eats, because the eating is not from faith.*

To eat or not to eat, that is the question. Paul's answer is, "You better be sure that you are right!" He leaves the people right there smack in the middle of the unknown to figure it out.

But Paul does not stop there. He takes things to an entirely new level in the second part of the verse. He expands this one unknown, this one gray area, to all the unknowns of life, writing,

*For whatever does not proceed from faith is sin.*

Paul is teaching a much bigger principle: when we are not sure, even if we guess right, we are not following God. Following God demands that we know what He wants us to do. Otherwise, we are not following Him at all. Embracing this standard, not doing a doubt, launches us into navigating the unknowns. It requires belief. It requires slow thinking. It requires waiting. And it requires the ability to synthesize God's principles and precepts throughout the Bible to navigate the unknown.

Disciples will face decisions where there is no clear biblical answer. There will be times that they cannot figure out what is going on. And in those times, they need to hear directly from God. It is the only way to be sure of what to do next. And it is precisely what God wants to do. Jesus said it this way,

> *"There is so much more I want to tell you, but you can't bear it now. $^{13}$When the Spirit of truth comes, he will guide you into all truth. He will not speak on his own but will tell you what he has heard. He will tell you about the future. $^{14}$He will bring me glory by telling you whatever he receives from me."*
> —John 16:12–14

Do you believe that Jesus is still active in our lives? Do you believe that the Spirit of God will guide us into all truth, not some truth but all truth? Do you believe that the Spirit can tell us about the future, our future? Jesus went further with these words:

> *"But when the Father sends the Advocate as my representa-tive—that is, the Holy Spirit—he will teach you everything and will remind you of everything I have told you."*
> —John 14:26

And now we see how important the Spirit is to facing the unknown. The Spirit is the key to knowing and understanding God's truths. The Spirit is the key to being confident and convinced, doing it on your own.

When we do not know what to do, when there is no clear biblical truth, the Spirit is ready to guide us, teach us everything, remind us of everything. The Spirit can even tell us our future! I love Jesus's words,

> *There is so much more I want to tell you, but you can't bear it now.*

Jesus did not tell his disciples everything. What were they supposed to do when they did not know what to do? How would they face the unknown? By listening to the Spirit of God, the voice of God. The disciples you make are no different. They can ask God questions and get definite answers to conquer the unknowns in life. They can know what God wants and be sure when facing into the gray. God does this through his Spirit, just like Jesus did in person with the disciples.

Disciples can hear directly from God. He can answer

them, convince them, and convict them. He can speak through burning bushes. More often, the Spirit speaks quietly in their hearts. His voice is the same voice that convicted them of right and wrong during preparation. It is the same voice that connected the dots and built their confidence. God also creates thought vacuums where disciples slow down, meditate on God's words helping them think and connect the dots. There are also times when God does not answer. Like a father answering a child's questions about where babies come from, God often holds details until we are mature enough to process them.

The Spirit of God is the disciple's answer to the unknowns. He longs to direct us. He longs to guide us, to protect us as we head off into the unknowns of life. The disciple's ability to hear from God without a priest, prophet, or you is the beginning of his success. Your work is to get him listening to the Spirit.

Each of our brains is powerfully designed by God. It stores, cross-references, and recalls data. It can process that data conceptually. It can use deductive reasoning to reach conclusions. You see that in Bedford. He is an automobile problem-solving machine. His deductive reasoning is a gift by God's design. Fueled by training, experiences, and his ability to connect the dots, Bedford can develop experiments to test his hypothesis and learn new things. He can do all this without listening to the Spirit. But that is not what Bedford does. Bedford prays through his problems.

Bedford is a believer, and he knows that the Spirit knows all things. He knows that the Spirit can empower his thinking. He understands God's design. Jesus told us that we could not understand the things of God without faith. Jesus' disciples got their answers to God's mysteries by asking Jesus directly. When Jesus left, God sent the Spirit to supercharge our ability to hear from God.

But the Spirit of God, the knowledge of God, is not limited to theological issues. He can tell us which hills are worth dying on. He can tell us which car to buy. He can tell us which deals will fall through, and he can help us discern what is going on deep inside a loved one. God has promised and demonstrated throughout time that he wants to guide us in the practical challenges of life. He wants to guide us through the unknowns.

Like Bedford, we have a lot of data already stored in our brains. We have access to the words of God recorded in the Bible. We can see examples of success and failure. We have the laws of God, which reflect his loving commandments. We have Paul deducing and explaining the mystery of Jesus. We know so much, and the Spirit uses what we know to help us navigate the unknown. However, when most of these events and truths were recorded, they were firsts. They were instances where the people of God had to figure out the unknown. Moses had to figure out where to get water in the desert. Solomon had to figure out how to be a young king. The apostles had to figure out how to lead a growing church.

Your final work in successfully making a disciple is to show him how to navigate the unknown, how to figure out what to do next when he has no clear direction, how to face the gray in his life.

Remind the disciple you are making that he is not alone as he faces the unknown.

*Trust in the LORD with all your heart; do not depend on your own understanding. <sup>6</sup>Seek his will in all you do, and he will show you which path to take.*
 —Proverbs 3:5–6

Remind her that she has access to all the knowledge and wisdom of God. It is there for the asking as long as she intends to act upon God's answers.

*If you need wisdom, ask our generous God, and he will give it to you. He will not rebuke you for asking. <sup>6</sup>But when you ask him, be sure that your faith is in God alone. Do not waver, for a person with divided loyalty is as unsettled as a wave in the sea that is blown and tossed by the wind. <sup>7</sup>Such people should not expect to receive anything from the Lord. <sup>8</sup>Their loyalty is divided between God and the world, and they are unstable in everything they do.*
 —James 1:5–8

Help the disciple you make learn to learn. Ask her which truths and histories "look and feel" similar to the decision or challenge she is facing. Prompt him as he learns to learn. Give him a clue when the riddle seems overwhelming. Then wait, pray, and let God's Spirit help him remember, learn, and connect the dots. Guide him to success.

Teach the disciple you make to believe in a practical God. When he cannot find his keys, ask him, "Have you prayed and asked God to inspire you or someone else where to look? Do you believe that God knows where your keys are?" I cannot tell you how many times I have used this exercise to launch disciples into believing in a practical God who actually knows everything. I cannot tell you how many times God has immediately come through, proving that, like a father, He wants to help.

Create unknowns along the way without telling the disciple what you are doing. Use this practice to prepare her for the unknowns she will face in the future. In essence, teach her how to solve a riddle. Ask her challenging questions like, "What is the difference between murdering and killing?" Once she solves that simple riddle, extend it to this question, "What is the difference between genocide and God protecting the Israelites by entirely wiping out their enemies?" The answer is found in extending the why from the first question to the second question.

Remind the disciple you make that God gives spiritual gifts to his children as they need those gifts. God helps his children discern, understand, and even lead.[2] He even gives practical gifts. I love how God gives craftsmen in the Old Testament a supernatural ability to be incredible at their trade.[3] Ask them, "Do you think God can help you be a better salesman?" or, "Can God help you figure out which deal to chase?" or, "Do you believe God can inspire your customer service?"

Your goal should not be answering all the unknowns. Neither do you have the time to do that nor can you know what they will face in the future. Your goal is to help them learn to learn. Your goal is to show them how to leverage God's design of memory and thinking with his agent, the Holy Spirit. Knowing what to do when it all seems gray does not require that they know everything. Navigating the unknown is about having the correct tools: the truth they know, the value of what they know, the big picture of who God is, and the Holy Spirit.

Your third measure of success, the final piece of making a disciple who thrives in this life, is the disciple navigating the unknowns.

# CHAPTER 10
# IT'S A WRAP

Your success in disciple making is measured by how many disciples continue to follow God for the right reasons and navigate the unknowns long after your influence fades. The intersection of these three measures will be where you find your lasting, successful investment.

In the intersection of prepared, confident, and skilled, opinion fades. The desire for solid, simple, God-given truths becomes the basis of life choices. Questions get answered. Confidence in God's ways and methods build. Disciples become successful in their lives and transform lives around them. They become walking, talking billboards reflecting God's glory by living out God's design for man. They have returned to God because He is God and live to be the very image of God. Simply put, they want to be like Him because that is God's original design for their success. And they believe in themselves and the Spirit of God within them.

You have succeeded in making a self-sustaining disciple. You can measure your success in each disciple you make. You can measure the success of your church's efforts. You can help others develop a plan that focuses on these three measures. But there is one more measure of your success. Your success will be measured in how many disciples you have made, are making, and plan to make.

*How many prepared, confident, and skilled disciples we make over time is also a measure of our success.*

I have purposefully avoided talking about numbers until now. In fact, you may have noticed that I often switched back to the singular writing, "the disciple you make." There are two reasons for my avoidance of this topic and my singular phrasing. First, you make individual disciples whenever you make a disciple, whether in small groups, larger groups, or one-on-one. No two people are the same. Their progress down the predictable pathway to spiritual maturity[1] will vary. Your approach with each disciple will need to be different. There is no cookie-cutter approach that well serves every disciple. Disciple making is more like art than factory work. You need to focus on each and every disciple you make. You make individual disciples.

The second reason I waited to talk about numbers is that our church systems are hopelessly geared to measuring success by numbers. We seem performance oriented in every area. Likewise, we tend to measure the wrong things when it comes to making disciples. We measure how many people are "in the program" and "through the program," giving little attention to whether we made prepared, confident, and skilled followers. We see statistics on how many leaders have been trained, how many people completed discipleship, and how many disciples are making disciples. But no one seems to be tracking what really matters: who those disciples are when we release them and how they perform after their release.

Nonetheless, how many well-made disciples I make is a measure of my success. God told me to do one thing: make disciples. This measure of success needs to be a part of my discipleship plan. How many have I made? How many am I making? Who is on my list to make next? These are all pertinent parts of my disciple-making plan. I am designed and designated by God to help people become followers of God.

God did not tell us to preach. He did not tell us to grow large churches. God did not tell us to run community programs. He did not tell us to have small groups. Granted, none of these ministries or goals are inherently bad. But they become harmful when they prevent us from making prepared, confident, and skilled followers. How many of us are so busy running churches, writing sermons, and managing ministries that we do not make even one disciple? God will not measure our ministry success by our preaching, speaking engagements, books, blogs, or leadership podcasts. He measures our ministry success by how many disciples we make—or should I say, how many we try to make?

*It is important to remember that people have the power of choice. Not everyone will choose to be a disciple. What do you do about that?*

Let me tell you a real story. A brokenhearted pastor in his forties was going through a divorce. Bob's wife chose to leave him. She had no real complaint—she just did not love him. Devastated, he turned to an older pastor, Carl, for help and guidance. Carl pointed him to 1 Timothy 3:1–8 and told the younger pastor that he needed to leave the ministry, saying, "You are no longer qualified."

"Wait, what did I do? I did nothing. She has no complaint against me. She just doesn't want to be with me."

"It doesn't matter, Bob," the older pastor said. "The Bible is clear. Leaders should be able to control their families, and you cannot control yours."

"But I have led my family well. My kids respect me. It's not like I can make her choose the correct path."

"Bob, I know you don't want to hear this," the old pastor continued. "If your wife goes out and shoots someone, you are responsible for her actions. You bought the gun. You bought the bullets. She is your responsibility."

Bob could not believe what he was hearing. How could this be his fault? He already felt like a failure. Now he was being told it was his fault. Depression set in, but that was not the end. Tom, one of Bob's young interns at his church, came to see him. Tom was a recent Bible school graduate looking for a church to lead.

"You know, Bob, I was thinking about what Carl said to you. I think he is right. It is your responsibility to lead her into righteousness. Clearly, you did not win that battle. How can you possibly lead others to Christ if you can't lead her? I mean, the scriptures are clear."

I know. The discussion sounds like something right out of the book of Job. Here is a guy with no known arguments against his character. He is serving God. He is doing his best. He cared for his wife. Heck, he loved her. Now his world is crashing around him, and the church, real people, are not only telling him he is a failure because of her choice, but they are also telling him it is his fault!

It took me many years to work through the passage of God's Word that those two men threw at Bob. It seemed on the surface that they had a point. It seemed pretty black and white. But something felt odd every time I read it.

*An overseer must be above reproach, the husband of one wife, sober-minded, self-controlled, respectable, hospitable, able to teach, [3]not a drunkard, not violent but gentle, not quarrelsome, not a lover of money. [4]He must manage his own household well, with all dignity keeping his children submissive, [5]for if someone does not know*

*how to manage his own household, how will he care for*
*God's church?*
　　—1 Timothy 3:2–5 (ESV)

Then it hit me like a ton of bricks. The requirement for Bob to lead was that he be a good family leader, that he know how to lead. If Bob led his wife well, if he was a good husband (which by even her words he was), how could her freedom to choose and her choice be his fault? She chose not to love. She chose not to follow God. She chose not to walk with him. How could it be his fault? If Bob was a failure because of her choice, then God was a failure too. Clearly, God Himself and the Holy Spirit could not win her over. And not just her, how many people throughout the millennia have turned their backs and walked away from God? Was Jesus a failure because people chose not to follow him? Is God a failure because people do not choose him? Clearly, the road to hell is wider than the road to heaven. Has God failed?

God is not failing when people choose not to follow him. You are not failing when people you try to make disciples choose not to follow God. You are not a failure when they walk away. You only fail when you do not try to make disciples or do a lousy job of making disciples.

But that is not you. You are capable. You care. So get a plan to make prepared, confident, and skilled followers. Change your work schedule and put more hours into discipleship than you do preaching. You do not need permission. God has called you. Do what is essential. Make disciples and make them well in a measurable way. Set a goal for how many disciples you will make this year.

Recruit a few people. Tell them your incredible story. Pitch the value. Promise them they will never be the same, and lead them on the most fantastic adventure through God's words.

One last piece of advice as you head off to make a disciple: stay out of his way, and stay out of God's way. Get him in the presence of God's Word and Spirit, and watch God make a disciple. There really is not much to do. Just walk with the disciple as he walks with God.

Good people do good things naturally. Help them be great by applying practical, God-given truths. Focus on who they are and are becoming, not on what they should do. The rest will follow. I promise.

# ABOUT US

## MAKING THE DISCIPLE THE HERO
## OF THEIR STORY

Sustainable Discipleship is a team, a model, and a movement.

We are discipleship nerds. We are passionate about success in disciple making—for us, but more importantly, for the disciples. We study discipleship. We have studied discipleship in the Bible. We rediscovered how God made and makes disciples. We study the work of others—their successes and failures. We study the results of our discipleship. We measure, we test, and we experiment with new discipleship ideas and techniques.

Our team's single focus is helping others achieve success in making self-sustaining, self-replicating disciples. In other words, we are focused on helping others do well the one thing that God told us to do: make disciples.

Our approach is different than most. Our team does not produce discipleship courses or promote a specific program. We help disciple makers become rock stars, making self-sustaining, self-replicating followers of God in their context: large, small, contemporary, or traditional. We do this by combining God's method with a clear under-standing of how people learn, think, and make decisions.

In other words, we make disciple makers and give them a simple, repeatable method to make more disciples than ever.

Sustainable Discipleship is also a movement of people passionate about helping Christians discover and live the abundant life that God promised. It is a movement to help people be prepared, confident, and skilled at following God. Churches of all denominations and characteristics are discovering passion, simplicity, and success in making disciples. Pastors and leaders are reaping the rewards. Disciples are succeeding.

If you want to talk discipleship, supercharge your disci-pleship, or join the movement, we are here. Sustainable Discipleship works. We guarantee it. And we have the data to back it up.

Doug
doug@sustainable-discipleship.com

# ABOUT THE AUTHOR

Doug Burrier is the founder of Different.ly, a decision science consulting firm that helps leaders, churches, and corporations make better decisions. Doug has a degree is decision sciences, a PhD in Christian leadership, and a master in biblical studies. He has researched, designed, and carried out discipleship for over twenty years as the pastor of Three Taverns Church, where he created the highly successful sustainable-discipleship model. Doug writes about discipleship from his home in Acworth, Georgia, where he lives with his wife and dog.

Doug is passionate about discipleship and regularly helps churches define and design successful disciple-making processes as a part of the Sustainable Discipleship's online learning, coaching, and private workshops. Doug is a high-energy, creative speaker. He thrives at unlocking the secrets of how to make and be disciples. To learn more or book Doug for your team or next event, email team@sustainable-discipleship.com.

# OTHER BOOKS AND RESOURCES

**How to Make Disciples: A Simple, Proven Model for Making Self-Sustaining Followers of God**

— Printed, ebook, and audio available on Amazon, Apple, Audible and at sustainable-discipleship.com/the-book

**Quick Smart Start: Sixteen Useful Truths for New Followers**

— A workbook. Printed. Available at sustainable-discipleship.com/resources and on Amazon.

**The Discipleship Pathway: Discovering the Highly Predictable Steps on the Way to Spiritual Maturity**

— Available at sustainable-discipleship.com

**Live Workshops: Be a Disciple-Making Superhero**

— Get started or hone your craft and become a disciple-making superhero with a public or private workshop. Increase involvement. Measure your success. Develop a clear, simple, repeatable plan. Host a workshop in your city.

— Learn more at sustainable-discipleship.com.

**Inspiration and Design Coaching**

Let us inspire your team, evaluate your process, or help you launch a sustainable-discipleship plan.

— Email us at team@sustainable-discipleship.com.

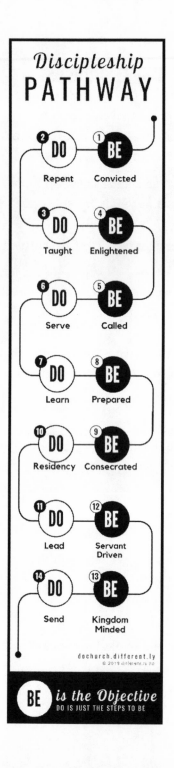

# NOTES

## 1. COCONUTS

1. God commanded Hosea to take "a wife of whoredom" in Hosea 1:2 (ESV), standing in opposition to his laws of sexual morality throughout the Old Testament. God also directly commanded the priests to not take a wife of whoredom in Leviticus 21:7. Though this law was specific for the priests, the spirit of this law seems consistent with the rest of God's laws and the spirit of those laws regarding sexual morality and marriage.

2. Opinions vary on whether David actually sinned by eating the bread of the altar (1 Samuel 21:1–6) that was reserved for the priests and their sons (Leviticus 24:5–9). Some claim that the priest had the right to share the bread that was "his bread." Others claim that the priest should not have given David the bread and that David should not have eaten the bread. The different interpretations arise because of Jesus' reference to the event when he explains to the Pharisees that the law was made for man and not man made for the law. Jesus makes this argument in reference to the Pharisees questioning him about healing and gleaning grain on the Sabbath. Some scholars believe that Jesus was pointing out the hypocrisy of the Pharisees as they questioned him for healing or gleaning on the Sabbath while they defended David for eating the altar bread. Other scholars argue that Jesus was comparing both actions, teaching that there are times when the welfare of man supersedes the letter of the law. For example, it was considered lawful to break the Sabbath to get your ox out of a ditch. Regardless of the interpretation, Jesus taught that the law was made for the benefit of man rather than the man made for the benefit of the law. There are times when the spirit of the law needs to be understood as if necessity supersedes the letter of the law.

3. Luke 21:1–4

4. Romans 12:1–2

5. Matthew 6:25–34

# 3. RIDDLE ME

1. John Anthony McGuckin, published by Shambhala, 2003.
2. Let me add a note of caution. We make disciples over three years and only use this resource in year three. It is complex and tends to distract or derail the less prepared.
3. 1 Timothy 4:7

# 4. SHEKEL SHACKLED

1. Random House Trade Paperbacks (January 7, 2014)

# 5. MINUS THREE, PLUS THREE

1. I talk about the Discipleship Pathway in a chapter of my book, *How to Make Disciples.* You can get a free copy of that chapter at sustainable-discipleship.com. An expanded version of that resource will be released in late 2021. The expanded version will include tips and tricks on what to do and what to look out for at each step along the pathway. You can get on the advanced notice list for the new resource by emailing team@sustainable-discipleship.com.

# 6. ELEPHANT

1. Asking, "Why is this an issue for you?" is powerful in discipleship. It helps keep disciples focused on truths that they can apply to their lives. People are prone to get distracted by hot topics (such as homosexuality, genocide, etc.) that in no way apply to their lives. Of course it is important to consume and understand God's truths on topics like these. However, if you aren't homosexual, then God's truths on homosexuality really have no power to transform your life. The secondary power of this question is that it often opens doors to areas of the disciple's life that need to be transformed. This allows you to help by pointing them to applicable truth.
2. To ignore sin in a disciple's life is to set them up for certain failure. Success in disciple making always calls people to follow. The difficulty is knowing where to draw the line. Throughout history, God has toler-

ated entire herds of elephants while He tried to make disciples. But when sin becomes defiant sin, God is done. God told the Israelites,

"But those who brazenly violate the LORD's will, whether native-born Israelites or foreigners, have blasphemed the LORD, and they must be cut off from the community. 31Since they have treated the LORD's word with contempt and deliberately disobeyed his command, they must be completely cut off and suffer the punishment for their guilt."

—Numbers 15:30–31

God has no tolerance for "in His face" sin. He has no tolerance when people look at Him and say, "I understand what you want, but I don't care. I am going to do it anyway." We should do everything possible to help a disciple avoid God's punishment. But when God is done, we need to create a necessary ending to discipleship and shift our strategy from discipleship to evangelism.

3. See the note from chapter five about discipleship checkpoints along the Predictable Pathway. Checkpoint nine is usually reached at the end of our second year of discipleship or at the beginning of discipleship three.

4. When I responded to Sally's email, I pushed her to reconcile Elephant with God's words. I warned her about the dangers of defiant sin. I asked her at what point she could no longer follow God and love her Elephant. Her answer was revealing.

"Do you think all disciples live out all truths? Is Sam less of a follower if I do not live out all truths? At what point does this extend? Would we be talking about this if I was not following in finances?

Without a doubt, we would be talking about finances if Sally was not following God's truths. The whole point of discipleship is to learn, understand, and apply God's truths—all of them. But Sally revealed something important: she realizes that she is not living out the truth by keeping Elephant.

Now that she knows Elephant is wrong, he might be the end to Sally's formal discipleship. She is at great danger of stalling at checkpoint nine, consecration. Consecration is that point where we go all in, where we will do whatever to follow God. If Sally is not willing to surrender Elephant to God's truth, it would be irresponsible and wasteful of everyone's time to continue with her final year of discipleship.

# 7. PREPARED

1. It is amazing to see how God used this same method while customizing it to each person's personality, learning style, fears, and circumstances. He reached Moses differently than Isaiah, Peter differently than Thomas, and the list goes on and on. You may want to check out the chapter on Customizing Discipleship in my book *How to Make Disciples*.

2. Excerpt from Doug Burrier, *How to Make Disciples: A Simple, Proven Model for Making Self-Sustaining Followers of God*.

3. Michelle Fabio, July 15, 2019, ThoughtCo.com, "How the Socratic Method Works and Why Is It Used in Law School."

4. Matthew 13:10–17, 2 Timothy 3:7

5. *Upstream: The Quest to Solve Problems Before They Happen*. Dan Heath, Avid Reader Press / Simon & Schuster (March 3, 2020).

6. Psalm 1:1–3, Psalm 119:15, and Philippians 4:8, among other verses.

7. Having disciples use a highlighter as they read is one of the most powerful tools in my discipleship toolbox. It allows them to quickly highlight or mark a truth and move on without getting disconnected from the stream of reading. It provides a simple way for them to be ready to discuss what the Holy Spirit showed them. Using a different color each time the disciple reads also filters out truths subconsciously, causing them to focus on verses and passages that they have not previously highlighted. If you would like to learn more about this powerful tool, reach out to me at doug@sustainable-discipleship.com.

# 8. CONFIDENT

1. You can read more about her journey in chapter seventeen of my book *How to Make Disciples*.

2. Eugene H. Peterson, *The Message: The Bible in Contemporary Language*. NavPress, 2005.

# 9. SKILLED

1. James 4:17, "Whoever knows the right thing to do and fails to do it, for him it is sin." (ESV)

2. Romans 12, 1 Corinthians 12

3. Exodus 31:1–5

# 10. IT'S A WRAP

1.  Did you know there is a fourteen-step, predictable pathway that every disciple travels from the beginning to spiritual maturity? You can read more in *How to Make Disciples*. The Predictable Pathway allows you to know exactly what to give each disciple at each moment to move them toward maturity.

38133018R00076